POST-SECO EDUCATION IN QATAR

EMPLOYER DEMAND, STUDENT CHOICE, AND OPTIONS FOR POLICY

G000135083

Cathleen Stasz · Eric R. Eide · Francisco Martorell

with

Louay Constant · Charles A. Goldman · Joy S. Moini
Vazha Nadareishvili · Hanine Salem

Prepared for the Supreme Education Council

RAND-QATAR POLICY INSTITUTE

The research described in this report was prepared for the Supreme Education Council and conducted within RAND Education and the RAND-Qatar Policy Institute, programs of the RAND Corporation.

Library of Congress Cataloging-in-Publication Data

Postsecondary education in Qatar : employer demand, student choice, and options for
  policy / Cathleen Stasz ... [et al.].
      p. cm.
  Includes bibliographical references.
  ISBN 978-0-8330-4173-9 (pbk.)
  1. Education, Higher—Qatar. 2. Higher education and state—Qatar.
I. Stasz, Cathleen, 1947–

LA1435.P67 2007
378.5363—dc22

                                                                2007017402

The RAND Corporation is a nonprofit research organization providing objective analysis and effective solutions that address the challenges facing the public and private sectors around the world. RAND's publications do not necessarily reflect the opinions of its research clients and sponsors.

RAND® is a registered trademark.

Published 2007 by the RAND Corporation
1776 Main Street, P.O. Box 2138, Santa Monica, CA 90407-2138
1200 South Hayes Street, Arlington, VA 22202-5050
4570 Fifth Avenue, Suite 600, Pittsburgh, PA 15213-2665
RAND URL: http://www.rand.org/
To order RAND documents or to obtain additional information, contact
Distribution Services: Telephone: (310) 451-7002;
Fax: (310) 451-6915; Email: order@rand.org

Preface

The government of Qatar is embarking on a number of reforms to support the nation's economic and social development. Qatar's future depends on citizens whose education and training prepare them to be full participants in economic, social, and political life, and Qatar has made significant efforts to improve educational opportunities. The efforts have included individual initiatives focused on post-secondary education, but these initiatives have not been subjected to a broad strategic review. Qatar's Supreme Education Council asked the RAND-Qatar Policy Institute to study the current situation and to help identify priorities for developing post-secondary educational offerings that better respond to the country's economic and social demands.

This monograph, which reports on the resulting one-year study, is written primarily for decisionmakers in Qatar. It may also be of interest to researchers and policymakers involved in higher education, as well as to those concerned with education and economic development in the Middle East.

This project was conducted under the auspices of the RAND-Qatar Policy Institute (RQPI) and RAND Corporation's Education unit. RQPI is a partnership of the RAND Corporation and the Qatar Foundation for Education, Science, and Community Development. The aim of RQPI is to offer the RAND style of rigorous and objective analysis to clients in the greater Middle East. In serving clients in the Middle East, RQPI draws on the full professional resources of the RAND Corporation. RAND Education analyzes education policy and practice and supports the implementation of improvements at all levels of the education system.

For further information on RQPI, contact the director, Dr. Richard Darilek. He can be reached by email at redar@rand.org; by telephone at +974-492-7400; or by mail at P.O. Box 23644, Doha, Qatar. For more information about RAND Education, contact the associate director, Dr. Charles Goldman. He can be reached by e-mail at charlesg@rand.org; by telephone at +1-310-393-0411, extension 6748; or by mail at RAND, 1776 Main Street, Santa Monica, California 90401 USA.

Contents

Figure

Tables

Summary

Like the government of many other countries, Qatar's government views education as a crucial element in the nation's economic, social, and political development. Qatar has embarked on reforms at all levels of its education system, the goal being to develop the human capital of Qatari nationals and to ensure that Qatar's citizens can contribute fully to society, both economically and socially.

Progress is being made, but Qatar still faces a number of challenges. The education system for kindergarten through grade 12 (K–12) does not adequately prepare Qataris for work or post-secondary study, and current reforms to the K–12 system will take time to bear fruit. The Qatari population is small, and the country depends on a large expatriate workforce for both low- and high-skilled labor. Few Qataris have the training or qualifications needed for high-demand, high-skill jobs. Employment practices, which are linked to the social welfare system, provide Qataris, especially men, with secure, well-compensated jobs in the government sector: Nearly 77 percent of employed Qataris work in the government or government enterprise sectors. And Qatari women, who are more highly educated than Qatari men, are less likely to pursue career employment and have limited employment opportunities because of cultural tradition.

Qatar has used its wealth to improve post-secondary educational opportunities—for example, by establishing a number of world-class institutions in Doha's Education City. But these efforts to enhance the quality of education have not undergone a broad strategic review. As a result, the extent to which available post-secondary educational offerings can meet Qatar's current and future demands remains uncertain.

Qatar's Supreme Education Council (SEC) asked RAND Education to analyze the current situation and to help articulate priorities for developing post-secondary educational opportunities, either in Qatar or through financed study abroad. The resulting one-year study addressed several questions:

1. In which occupations can Qataris make the greatest contribution to the society and economy, and what education and training are needed to realize these contributions?
2. What measures might encourage more Qataris, especially young men, to pursue post-secondary education?
3. To what extent do existing institutions meet education and training needs? Are new investments required, and if so, where?
4. What are the benefits and costs of establishing local post-secondary institutions at the undergraduate and graduate levels versus sending students abroad for these studies?

Data and Methods

We used a combination of qualitative and quantitative research methods for the study. To address issues of occupation and skill demand, our research team reviewed secondary data and research from Qatar's Planning Council, formally interviewed key employers in Qatar, and informally discussed relevant issues with other education stakeholders.

The study team also inventoried the post-secondary educational offerings in Qatar, including private training organizations, and obtained data on Qatar's scholarship programs, which support high-achieving students studying in Qatar and abroad.

Many decisionmakers in Qatar recognize that the education and employment choices made by Qataris are often not well aligned with Qatar's new national priorities and initiatives, but evidence for why these choices are made has been mostly anecdotal. To shed light on the factors influencing education and employment choices, we used two surveys to gather systematic data that allowed us to generalize: a telephone survey of 99 Qataris who had graduated from secondary school in 1998, and a survey administered to 260 students who were secondary school seniors in 2006. The survey of the 1998 graduates provided a look at the transition to post-secondary education and employment in the eight years following graduation from secondary school; the survey of the 2006 seniors provided information on education and employment aspirations and the factors influencing those aspirations.

Findings

Demands for Education and Employment

Our employer interviews and data from Qatar's Planning Council indicate that demands for men are in the professional, technical, and sales and service occupations and that women are more likely to find employment in clerical jobs and in professional jobs within the government. Overall, the pattern of occupational demand favors individuals with some post-secondary education supplemented with more-specific job training.

Survey data from our study align with Qatar's 2004 census data in indicating that patterns of education and employment among Qataris are somewhat misaligned with demand. This is especially true for males: Qatari men continue to pursue careers in fields other than those in demand—most notably the military and police—and a majority of the male students surveyed aspire to these professions. As for Qatari females, a high proportion are in the teaching profession, about 15 percent of the Qatari women surveyed hold professional jobs, and a high proportion of the female students surveyed aspire to be managers or professionals rather than teachers. Women's opportunities appear to be expanding, but cultural expectations may still work against women's employment in some fields.

The trend for Qatari females to pursue and achieve a post-secondary education in greater proportions than Qatari men will likely continue given that twice as many female students as male students indicated that they plan to attend a university or obtain a post-secondary diploma.

While government policy aims to increase Qataris' employment in the growing private sector, the trend for Qataris to work for or seek work in the government or government enterprises will likely continue.

Employers showed a high demand for people skilled in certain areas, especially English, information and communication technology (ICT), and business. They also value the so-called soft skills, such as a good work attitude and a willingness to learn. By and large, employers indicated dissatisfaction with the skills of secondary school and university graduates; they also pointed out several shortcomings of Qataris compared with expatriate workers with respect to attitudes toward work.

We found that many factors influence education and employment choices and aspirations, and that these factors often vary for males versus females and for older versus younger people. For example, in making post-secondary education and career choices, students are highly influenced by parents and religious beliefs. While our findings about these factors are in no way conclusive, they do provide important insights for policymakers.

Qataris Who Do Not Pursue Post-Secondary Study

Even though economic demands in Qatar favor individuals with post-secondary education and training, a majority of Qataris do not pursue post-secondary studies. What might induce more Qataris, especially Qatari males, to do so? To isolate factors that might underlie the decision to pursue an education at the post-secondary level, we used census data and data from our surveys to compare the characteristics and experiences of Qataris who had decided to pursue a post-secondary education with those of Qataris who had decided not to.

Our survey results highlight several factors involved in this complex decision. These findings are somewhat speculative, however, because the sample sizes in some of the comparisons were small. With this caveat, we can state that the most common reasons for not pursuing a post-secondary education are ineligibility for a scholarship and family responsibilities. Because scholarships are attached to grades in Qatar, what this effectively means is that a student's poor performance in secondary school is a significant barrier to further study. For these individuals, opportunities for remedial education may have appeal and may be of benefit for bringing more students into post-secondary education.

Workers without a post-secondary education viewed additional training in English and, to a lesser extent, basic computer skills as helpful for either advancing in their current job or getting a better job in the future. These views align with the skill demands indicated by employers.

Secondary school seniors who do not plan to pursue post-secondary studies are more likely to want to work in a government ministry and less likely to go on to work in a government-owned or privately owned company than are those who intend to continue their studies. This suggests that the availability of secure, prestigious, and well-paying government jobs that do not require post-secondary schooling may act as a disincentive to pursuing further education, especially for Qatari males. In this case, changes in educational opportunities alone may not be sufficient for altering the patterns of those choosing not to pursue post-secondary studies.

Adequacy of Post-Secondary Education and Training Offerings

Our analysis of the opportunities available in Qatar for post-secondary education in high-demand fields indicated that there are numerous relevant offerings at the certificate/diploma level and undergraduate-degree level. It also indicated that there are very few offerings at the graduate level in any field. However, Qatar's Higher Education Institute offers numerous scholarship opportunities for students of different abilities who want to study abroad, where such offerings are available, and some of these scholarships target preparation for high-demand occupations.

One part of our review identified a large number of organizations in Qatar that provide training, including training in specific skills highly valued in the labor market, such as English and ICT. The opportunities for this type of training thus seem plentiful, although our study did not attempt to assess the quality of the training being offered.

We found that the post-secondary offerings in Qatar provide good coverage of high-demand fields at some levels but that there were notable gaps:

- Opportunities for students who need remedial academic course work are limited.
- High-quality degree choices in Qatar are limited.
- Opportunities to study for a master's degree are limited.

These gaps have different effects on men and women, on recent secondary school graduates and those who have been out of school awhile, and on students considered and not considered highly able.

Options for Post-Secondary Investment and Our Recommendations

For each gap in Qatar's educational offerings, we outlined the conceptual costs and benefits of three post-secondary investment options of interest to the SEC: (1) restructure programs at Qatar University, (2) recruit new foreign institutions to Qatar, and (3) develop new government-sponsored programs of less than four years.

Based on our study, we recommend that Qatari leadership consider the following investments for the three gaps in its post-secondary offerings:

- Gap: Limited opportunities for remedial course work prior to university study
  - Option: Establish a government-sponsored community college

  Addressing this gap will benefit remedial and adult students.

- Gap: Limited four-year degree choices for high-achieving students in Qatar beyond the Education City offerings
  - Option: Recruit a top liberal arts college to Education City
  - Option: Develop an honors program at Qatar University

  Addressing this gap will benefit high-achieving students.

- Gap: Lack of master's degrees in career-related fields in Qatar
  - Option: Expand offerings of current Education City campuses to include master's degrees in career-related fields
  - Option: Restructure Qatar University programs to begin offering more master's degrees in career-related fields

Addressing this gap will benefit high-achieving students.

We also recommend that a financial-aid program for adults be developed to help finance their post-secondary education and training.

Another recommendation is that Qatari decisionmakers not invest in any of these areas without first prioritizing the post-secondary gaps according to their importance to the economy and society. The issues to consider here include the extent to which an option addresses areas of national significance in terms of furthering Qatar's economic and social goals, the number and type of individuals who will benefit from investment in an option, and the trade-offs between study in Qatar and study abroad. For example, providing high-quality graduate training in Qatar will go a long way toward developing future leaders for the country, particularly women.

In addition, we recommend that the SEC conduct further feasibility studies to determine in detail what is involved in investing in the areas of highest priority. It will also be necessary to estimate the demand for post-secondary education related to each option.

We further recommend that a national campaign be conducted to raise awareness of the importance of higher education and the occupational areas that will aid economic development. This campaign should be directed both at parents, because they have much influence over their children's education and career choices, and at adults that might want to resume their schooling, upgrade their English or ICT skills, or further educate themselves as a way to advance in their current job or expand their employment opportunities.

In going forward with these recommendations, it is crucial that a long-term, overarching strategy of investment be developed for post-secondary education in Qatar, one that coordinates the various educational institutions and considers related policy areas, especially those of employment and labor. At present, Qataris continue to pursue traditional occupational pathways in government ministries despite the availability of ample opportunities for post-secondary education and training in high-demand occupations. While the factors that influence people's education and career choices are complex, it is clear that these decisions are to some degree influenced by Qatar's employment policies and customs—for example, the virtual guarantee that Qatari men with no more than a secondary school education will find secure, well-paying, and prestigious jobs in Qatar's government ministries. Another influencing factor may be the limited educational and employment opportunities that exist for women. Any post-secondary investment strategy needs to be framed within a larger context that takes these factors into consideration. Only in this way will policymakers be able to understand the range of incentives likely to be influencing individual choices and thus be able to make the best investments for future generations of Qataris.

Acknowledgments

This project would not have been possible without the cooperation of many individuals and organizations. First, we thank the Supreme Education Council (SEC), which provided full support to this project and helped us gain access to schools, employers, and other organizations.

Early in the project we met with a number of individuals to discuss the broad scope of the study and to share views on education and employment issues in Qatar. We thank Ms. Sabah Al Haidoos, Dr. Hind Jolo, Dr. Sheikha Bin Jabor Al Thani, Mr. Mohammad Al Manaa, Sheik Hamad Bin Jabor Al Thani, Dr. Abdullah Al Thani, and Mr. Ibrahim Al Ghussein for their time and interest in the study.

Many organizations agreed to participate in formal interviews: Hamad Medical Corporation, Qatar Petroleum, the SEC's Education and Evaluation Institutes, Sheraton Hotel Doha, Qatar National Bank, Qatar Airways, Qatar Armed Forces, Ministry of the Interior, Ministry of Civil Services and Housing, and Supreme Council of Information and Communication Technology. We thank their representatives for providing candid and thoughtful responses to our confidential interview questions.

Several organizations provided information about their post-secondary programs. The higher education institutions were Virginia Commonwealth University–Qatar, Weill Cornell Medical College–Qatar, Georgetown University–Qatar, CHN University Netherlands–Qatar, College of the North Atlantic–Qatar, and Qatar University. Private-training providers also kindly responded to our requests for information: New Horizons, ELS Language Centers, the British

Council, Expert, and Hi Tech. We thank Dr. Jehan Al Meer, Director of the Higher Education Institute, for providing data and other information on Qatar's scholarship programs.

Finally, we thank the individuals who participated in the anonymous telephone interviews and surveys.

A large international team carried out this research, and the team's collective work contributed to this report. In Doha, Hanine Salem organized the fieldwork for the survey of those who had graduated from secondary school in 1998, which was most ably carried out within a very short time frame by Eiman Al Ansari, Hessa Al Thani, Abdulrazaq Al Kuwari, Mie Al Missned, and Louay Constant. Louay Constant identified schools and respondents for the survey of secondary school seniors in 2006 and, along with Eiman Al Ansari, Mie Al Missned, Joy Moini, Hanine Salem, and Abdulrazaq Al Kuwari, administered the survey. Joy Moini spearheaded the collection of data for the inventory of post-secondary education and training offerings. Lawrence Tingson helped with data organization. In the RAND Santa Monica office, Vazha Nadareishvili analyzed the survey data while Mirka Vuollo and Kayla Ferguson analyzed the interviews. Dell Felder and Mirka Vuollo focused on issues concerning women in the workforce. Charles Goldman, associate director of RAND Education, provided thoughtful input throughout the study. Sharon Koga carried out various administrative duties. Christopher Dirks helped with document production.

RAND colleagues Laura Hamilton and Sue Bodilly provided helpful comments on an initial draft of this report. The final report, presented here, was greatly improved by the thoughtful comments and suggestions of two formal reviewers, Tora Bikson and Dominic Brewer.

Abbreviations

B.A.	bachelor of arts (degree)
GCC	Gulf Cooperation Council
HEI	Higher Education Institute
IAD	Institute of Administrative Development
ICDL	International Computer Driving License
ICT	information and communication technology
ISCO	International Standard Classification of Occupations
IT	information technology
K–12	kindergarten through grade 12
M.D.	doctor of medicine (degree)
MRSM	Manpower Requirements Simulation Model
MoCSAH	Ministry of Civil Service Affairs and Housing
Ph.D.	doctor of philosophy (degree)
QAR	Qatari Riyals
RQPI	RAND-Qatar Policy Institute
SEC	Supreme Education Council
USD	U.S. dollars

CHAPTER ONE

Introduction

The Arabian Gulf nation of Qatar is one of the smallest of the Gulf States, but its significant oil and natural gas reserves make it one of the wealthiest countries in the world. Qatar's progressive leadership is aiming to diversify the country's economy, with an emphasis on creating a dynamic private sector and increasing employment opportunities for Qataris. The leadership is also promoting social and political reforms to expand the role of Qatari women in society and, through a new constitution, move the country toward democratic institutions. Like the leaders of many other nations, Qatar's leaders recognize that education is key to economic, social, and political progress.

Qatar has chosen to invest its wealth in education and has already made significant efforts to improve its post-secondary educational opportunities. The Qatar Foundation for Education, Science, and Community Development (commonly called the Qatar Foundation) is responsible for a number of world-class institutions (e.g., Weill Cornell Medical College, Carnegie Mellon University) having established campuses in Qatar's Education City, and thus for expanding local options for post-secondary education. Qatar University has initiated both organizational and curricular reforms. The Higher Education Institute (HEI) of the Supreme Education Council (SEC) is revamping the available scholarship offerings to help ensure that students who study abroad attend top-ranked programs in the world's best colleges and universities. The objective of these and other efforts is to advance the quality of higher education in Qatar and to develop the human resources needed to continue Qatar's ambitious goals for social and economic development.

Despite these efforts, however, Qatar faces significant barriers to progress:

- Qatar's K–12 (kindergarten through grade 12) education system is weak, which means that students are poorly prepared for post-secondary study. The SEC has embarked on an ambitious reform of K–12 schooling, one that holds promise for better preparing graduates for higher education and work, but it began in 2001 and will require more time to yield significant effects (Brewer et al., 2007).
- Qatar depends on an expatriate workforce for both low-skilled labor and high-skilled technicians, managers, and professionals, especially for the energy sector. Most Qataris do not have the training or qualifications required for many high-demand, high-skill jobs in the expanding economy (Planning Council, 2005).
- An implicit social contract guarantees Qataris employment in the government sector, which employs about 77 percent of all Qataris in the workforce. Qataris favor work in government jobs, which provide them with high salaries and good benefits, short working hours, job security, and little competition from expatriates better qualified than they are (Planning Council, 2002, 2005).
- "Qatarization" policies directed at increasing Qatari employment in the energy sector and the private sector do not always succeed, because many Qataris are not willing or lack the needed skills to work in these sectors (Planning Council, 2005).
- Compared with Qatari males, Qatari females are higher academic achievers but are less likely to pursue career employment and are subject to cultural traditions that limit their job opportunities. Qatari males tend to be academically unmotivated but have high expectations about securing respectable jobs.
- Qatar lacks a mechanism for coordinating workforce development, including education and training, to rectify skill shortages and other imbalances in the labor market (Planning Council, 2005).

Given these barriers, the most pressing problem for Qatar's leadership is that of determining what kinds of initiatives will best broaden and strengthen Qatari participation in post-secondary education. Individual initiatives already carried out have paved the way for establishing a range of post-secondary educational opportunities in Qatar, but these initiatives have not been subjected to a broad strategic review. As a result, the extent to which available post-secondary educational offerings meet Qatar's current and future economic needs is uncertain.

The SEC asked the RAND Corporation to study the current situation and to help develop priorities for providing the needed post-secondary offerings, either in Qatar or by financing the education of Qataris abroad. The purpose of the RAND study was twofold: to provide a basis upon which to develop a more strategic approach to post-secondary education, and to address the issues and options in an integrated fashion.

We conducted a one-year study, beginning in November 2005; it addressed four main questions:

1. In which occupations can Qataris contribute most to the society and economy, and what education and training do they need to be able to make these contributions?
2. What measures might encourage more Qataris, especially young Qatari males, to pursue post-secondary education?
3. To what extent do existing post-secondary institutions meet the education and training needs? Are new investments required; if so, where?
4. What are the benefit and cost trade-offs between establishing local post-secondary institutions and sending students to study abroad?

Because recent policies and social forces in Qatar have sought to increase women's potential and their participation in the economic sphere, we paid particular attention to the issue of women in the workforce as we addressed these questions.

Data and Methods

We used a combination of qualitative and quantitative research methods and data sources in this study. To develop a more detailed understanding of which occupations and skills are the most valuable now and into the future, we interviewed key employers in the public and private sectors. We asked them about their skill needs, the quality of graduates from current educational institutions, their training and recruitment strategies, and other topics. In all, we conducted formal interviews with 18 individuals from ten employer organizations. We also held informal meetings with about ten other education stakeholders to discuss a number of broader issues relevant to the study.

We surveyed 99 Qatari nationals (49 women and 50 men) who had graduated from secondary school in 1998 in order to learn about the employment and education choices they had made since then. We used a random sample, drawn from records provided by the Ministry of Education, that included individuals not currently in the labor market in order to learn what factors had influenced their decision not to work. The sample was designed to represent both men and women who had specialized in each of the main fields of study in secondary school.

We also surveyed 260 secondary school seniors (154 women and 106 men) to learn about their education and employment aspirations and the factors influencing their goals and choices. For this survey, we used a randomly selected sample of schools (one private and nine government schools).

To analyze these data, we compared sample means and proportions across different groups identified in the data. For instance, we extensively compared males' and females' responses and, because of the particular relevance to policymakers, the responses of individuals who did and who did not pursue post-secondary schooling. Where appropriate, we used standard statistical tests (e.g., t-test, chi-square test) to determine whether differences across groups were statistically significant. Results were weighted to reflect population characteristics.

The surveys carried out in this study represent an important source of data because they capture essential insights about the factors that influence Qataris' education and employment choices. To date, decisionmakers have had to rely mainly on anecdotal evidence about factors that may drive individual choices. A better understanding of these factors should help decisionmakers craft policies and incentives that will more effectively direct education and employment choices in ways that support Qatar's broader economic and social goals.

The study also incorporated various secondary data sources. We used data from Qatar's 2004 census (Planning Council, 2004) and from two studies conducted by Qatar's Planning Council (2002, 2005) to examine characteristics of the workforce—e.g., distribution of the workforce by gender, nationality (Qatari, non-Qatari), industry, occupation, and educational credential. These data shed light on who works in occupations considered vital to Qatar's economy and society and who will work in such occupations in the future.

To supplement the surveys and interviews, we also reviewed information on education, employment, training, and skill needs that was available from numerous prior and ongoing RAND studies. Drawing on this information was a way to reduce the need to re-interview institutions and individuals previously visited.

Finally, we contacted post-secondary education and training institutions in Qatar to gather information, through questionnaires and interviews, about course offerings, students, and the like in order to compile an inventory of available offerings. We also obtained data from the Higher Education Institute on enrollment in various government-sponsored scholarship programs.

Study Limitations

This study relied on secondary data from Qatar's Planning Council, supplemented by interviews with a sample of key employers, to paint a broad picture of the demand for occupations and skills in Qatar. The Planning Council analyses are somewhat limited because of a lack of data in Qatar. In addition, the economic picture changes quite rapidly in Qatar, so even when data are available, they are not always up to date. In consequence, we were unable to make precise numerical estimates about demands, which in turn affected our analysis of whether Qatar provides adequate educational opportunities.

We did not attempt to carry out a complete inventory of the many training establishments in Qatar that might contribute to developing Qatar's human capital. The study's short time frame and the lack of centralized, systematic information or data on providers prohibited us from performing a detailed analysis of this education and training sector.

Monograph Organization

Chapter Two provides brief background information on Qatar, its labor market, and the policy context that informed the direction of our study. Chapters Three through Six are organized according to the study questions. Chapter Three addresses the skill and occupational demands in Qatar and the education and training needed to meet those demands. It examines the patterns of education and employment of two cohorts of Qataris—year 1998 secondary school graduates and year 2006 secondary school seniors—to determine whether these patterns reflect demands.

Chapter Four focuses on the characteristics and outcomes for Qataris who do not pursue a post-secondary education—a group of particular concern to policymakers. Chapter Five describes the current provision of education and training in Qatar and addresses the issue of whether it is sufficient for Qatar's current and future needs. Chapter Six outlines the options, based on our cost-benefit analysis, for expanding post-secondary opportunities in Qatar. Chapter Seven summarizes our recommendations.

Three appendixes are also provided. Appendix A contains further details on the study approach and methods; Appendixes B and C provide additional information on the provision of, respectively, post-secondary education and training in Qatar.

CHAPTER TWO

Overview of Qatar and the Policy Context

The Arabian Gulf nation of Qatar is only 11,427 square kilometers in area (similar in size to the U.S. state of Connecticut), but its significant oil and natural gas reserves and its strategic location and progressive leadership give it a unique status in today's world.

This chapter provides relevant background information on Qatar's population, education system, economy and industry, and labor force to provide context for our study. In doing so, it touches on the broad policy context, especially as it affects education and employment.

Brief History[1]

Qatar is a relatively new country, having made the shift from tribal community to modern state in a matter of decades. Most Qataris are Arabs and virtually all are Muslim, with the vast majority following Wahhabi Islam, a traditional version of Sunni Islam (Economist Intelligence Unit, 2004). Arabic is the primary language spoken and the official language of the government, but English is widely spoken and commonly used in business, especially in the private sector. Islam is the state's official religion.

Qatar became a sovereign state only recently. At the beginning of the 20th century, the territory now known as Qatar consisted of a small set of villages dependent on pearl diving, camel breeding, and

---

[1] This overview draws on material presented in an earlier RAND study on Qatar's K–12 education system (Brewer et al., 2007).

fishing, and its society was governed by Islamic principles and tribal custom. In 1916, Abdullah Bin Ali Al Thani, the leader of a prominent family, signed a treaty for Qatar to become a British Protectorate, as did other Gulf States at this time. In exchange for military protection, Qatar relinquished autonomy in foreign affairs. Britain terminated treaty arrangements with the Gulf States in 1968, and Qatar became an independent state on September 3, 1971. Soon after it proclaimed independence, Qatar became a member of the United Nations and the Arab League.

The ruling Al Thani family has been prominent in Qatari society since the late 1880s. In 1972, Sheikh Kalifa Bin Hamad took control from the Emir, Sheikh Ahmad Bin Ali, with support from the Al Thani family, Britain, and Saudi Arabia. He ruled until 1995, when Sheikh Hamad Bin Kalifa, the heir apparent and minister of defense at the time, took over from his father.

In 1972, the government was structured as a monarchy with a provisional constitution granting full legislative and executive powers to the head of state. A council of ministers, appointed by the Emir, had responsibility for drafting legislation, supervising implementation of the law, running financial and administrative systems, and preparing development plans. An advisory council was established, as a partially elected consultative body, with members selected from representatives chosen through a limited electoral process. This structure remained relatively unchanged until Sheikh Hamad initiated more progressive reforms geared toward developing a democracy.

In 1998, the Emir issued a decree setting up the framework for an elected municipal council of 29 members, for which both men and women could run and vote. By 2003, this council included one elected female member. In 1999, the Emir established a 32-member commission to develop a draft constitution specifying an elected parliament with legislative powers. A permanent constitution was ratified in April 2003. Although considerable powers remain with the ruling Al Thani family, the Advisory Council is to be expanded to 45 members, 30 elected and 15 appointed by the Emir. Voting is to be universal for all Qatari citizens over the age of 18. The constitution also guarantees freedom of expression, press, and religion, as well as the right of citizens to assemble and to establish civic and professional associations.

Social reforms have also been initiated in Qatar, some with the assistance of the Emir's wife, Her Highness Sheikha Mozah Bint Nassar Al Missned. Sheikha Mozah has been actively involved in developing educational opportunities through the Qatar Foundation, a private, non-profit organization whose board of directors she chairs. One of these developments, the establishment of Education City, is discussed further in Chapter Five.

Since the 1950s, income from oil has enabled Qatar to provide its citizens with social welfare benefits. The government provides free education and health care to all Qatari citizens. Family allowances for each child are granted to male heads of households employed in the public sector. In accordance with Qatari Social Security Law, monthly allowances are paid to widows, divorcees, orphans, and those with special needs who have no providers. Free land and interest-free construction loans for residential houses are provided to Qataris who work as senior staff in government and semi-government offices. Houses are constructed for Qataris with limited incomes who agree to pay back 60 percent of the cost over 20 to 25 years (Nafi, 1983).

Non-citizens, a group that includes persons who have lived in Qatar their entire lives or were born in Qatar (to non-citizen parents), are not eligible for the government benefits provided to citizens. With few exceptions, only Qataris are permitted to own land, and companies operating in Qatar must be at least 51 percent Qatari owned (U.S. Library of Congress, 1994). However, non-citizens do benefit from the fact that water, electricity, and gas are extremely inexpensive; some basic foods are subsidized; local telephone calls are free; employees pay no income tax; and no one pays property or municipal taxes.

Population

Qatar's demographics exhibit three striking features that must be seriously considered in developing any post-secondary education strategy. First, although Qatar's total population is small—just under 750,000 at the time of the 2004 census (Planning Council, 2004)—it has grown rapidly in recent years. Since 1986, the population of Qatar has more than doubled. The implied annual population growth rate of just over 4 percent is faster than any country currently experiences (Central Intelligence Agency, 2007). This rapid growth mirrors the economic boom in Qatar and the other Gulf States (Institute of International Finance, Inc., 2006). The U.S. Census Bureau's projections indicate that Qatar's population will continue to grow rapidly, exceeding 1.1 million people by 2020.

The second striking demographic feature, which can be seen in Table 2.1, is the preponderance of non-Qataris living in the country. In terms of individuals age 15 and over, non-Qataris constitute more than four-fifths of the population. Most non-Qataris are migrants who come mainly from Asian countries unable to offer the economic opportunities available in Qatar. Government policies (such as Qatarization, which is discussed below) intended to reduce Qatar's reliance on foreign workers have not reduced this large presence (Winckler, 2000). Qatar's share of expatriate workers remains significantly larger than that of Bahrain, Oman, and Saudi Arabia; and of all the Gulf Cooperation Council (GCC) countries, only Qatar and Oman have seen no reduction in their expatriate labor force in the past five years (Planning Council, 2005, Fig. 2.3). It is significant that if the population of non-Qataris were to be reduced, the Qatari population would not be large enough to fill all the jobs in Qatar's rapidly expanding economy (Planning Council, 2005).

Qatar's third striking demographic feature, which can also be seen in Table 2.1, is that males substantially outnumber females. Among

Table 2.1
Qatari and Non-Qatari Populations, Age 15 and Over, by Gender

	Number (Percentage)		
	Qataris	Non-Qataris	Total
Male	54,482 (13.2)	356,734 (86.8)	411,216
Female	55,923 (33.9)	109,272 (66.1)	165,195
Total	110,405	466,006	

SOURCE: Planning Council, 2004.

individuals age 15 and over, males make up about 70 percent of the population. This is not surprising given that non-Qataris are the majority in the population, most non-Qataris are migrants who came to Qatar to work, and migrant workers tend to be male. Among Qataris, there is no gender imbalance. Instead, there is approximate parity between the numbers of men and women.

Education

Before oil was discovered and the subsequent economic boom began transforming Qatar into one of the wealthiest countries in the world, opportunities for formal education were few. Some children memorized passages from the Qur'an and learned to read and write in a *kuttab* (an informal class taught in a mosque or home by a literate man or woman knowledgeable about Islam) (U.S. Library of Congress, 1994). With the establishment of Qatar's Ministry of Education in 1956, however, free education was provided for boys and girls, and Qatari students received a monthly stipend from that year until 1962. In addition, children of expatriates employed by the government became eligible for free education.

The Ministry of Education schools are divided into three levels: primary (grades 1–6), preparatory (grades 7–9), and secondary (grades 10–12). Boys and girls attend separate schools, taught, respectively, by male and female teachers.[2] Tuition-based private schools serve both Qataris and resident expatriates. Private Arabic schools follow the Ministry's curriculum and are geared toward Qataris and other Arabs who want their children's schooling to follow the national curriculum but take place in a private school setting. Other private schools follow curricula from other countries; for example, the elite Qatar Academy offers the International Baccalaureate (IB) program, and Doha College follows the British curriculum.

---

[2]   Women also teach boys up to grade 4 in "model schools" that were established to provide more employment opportunities for female teachers and to ease the home-to-school transition for young boys.

In recent years, Qatari leaders became concerned that Qatar's K–12 education system was not producing high-quality outcomes and that the system was not only rigid and outdated, but also resistant to reform. In 2001, Qatar embarked on a major reform effort to better align the system with the country's changing economic, social, and political ambitions (Brewer et al., 2007). The intent is that the reform will produce Qatari students who are better prepared for post-secondary education and for employment. However, it is still too soon for the reform's intended effects to be realized.

Qatar University, the nation's only state-sponsored, academically oriented institution, was established in 1977; it currently offers six fields of study: Humanities, Education, Sciences, Sharia and Law, Business Administration and Economics, and Engineering. Before 2000, Qatar University's College of Education offered undergraduate teaching degrees, and most Qatari public school teachers trained there. Degrees in general education are now no longer offered, although students can still pursue a bachelor of arts (B.A.) degree in arts or physical education or can secure a diploma in special or early-childhood education. In 2003, Qatar University began a reform effort to articulate both a new vision and a new mission and to develop a plan for realizing them (Qatar University, 2006). In addition, the government established a scholarship program to assist qualified students who want to study abroad.

Since 1995, the Qatar Foundation has brought world-class universities to Qatar's Education City—for example, Weill Cornell Medical College, Carnegie Mellon University, and Georgetown University all operate campuses there. The presence of these institutions in Qatar provides further educational opportunities for Qataris at the post-secondary level. (Chapter Five provides more information about Qatar University, Education City, and scholarship programs.)

At the time of Qatar's 1970 census, more than two-thirds of the population over 15 years of age was illiterate (Winckler, 2000). The significant investments made in the education infrastructure since then have paid off. For example, literacy rates increased through the years, reaching 98.2 percent among 15–19 year olds in 2004 (Planning Council, 2005). However, although Qatar compares relatively favorably with other Arab countries on student enrollment in primary and preparatory schools, its standing is below that of many others on enrollment in pre-primary schools and in higher education (Planning Council, 2005).

The disparities in levels of educational attainment for Qataris and non-Qataris, the old and the young, and men and women are significant. Table 2.2 shows educational attainment by gender for Qataris and non-Qataris. As can be seen, Qataris are better educated than non-Qataris on average: 53 percent of Qataris have at least a secondary degree, compared with 39 percent of non-Qataris. However, it can also be seen that a sizable group, 22 percent, of non-Qataris have some education beyond secondary school, and 17 percent have at least a university degree. The data in this table also show that women are better educated than men: 31 percent of women have some post-secondary schooling, compared with 21 percent of men. Among Qataris alone, 31 percent of women and 27 percent of men have some post-secondary schooling.

Table 2.3 uses tabulations from the 2004 census (Planning Council, 2004) to separately examine levels of schooling for Qataris

Table 2.2
Educational Attainment of Qataris and Non-Qataris, by Gender

	Percent Attaining Education Level		
	Less Than Secondary	Secondary	Beyond Secondary
Qatari			
Males	50	23	27
Females	45	24	31
Total	48	24	29
Non-Qatari			
Males	65	15	20
Females	47	22	31
Total	61	17	22
All males	63	16	21
All females	47	23	31
Total	59	18	23

SOURCE: Planning Council, 2004.

Table 2.3
Educational Attainment of Qataris Age 25 and Over, by Age Group and Gender

	Percent Attaining Education Level					
	Females			Males		
Age Group	Less Than Secondary	Secondary	Beyond Secondary	Less Than Secondary	Secondary	Beyond Secondary
25–29	26	29	46	43	30	26
30–34	30	20	50	41	21	38
35–39	38	17	46	44	19	38
40–44	47	13	39	41	17	42
45–49	62	10	28	45	14	40
50–54	84	6	10	49	15	36
55–59	94	3	3	68	12	20
60–64	97	1	2	83	8	9
65–69	99	1	1	90	5	5
70–74	99	0	1	93	3	3
75+	99	0	1	97	1	2
Total	50	15	35	50	19	32

SOURCE: Planning Council, 2004.

age 25 and older by age group and gender.[3] The results show that the older groups, which came of age when fewer educational opportunities existed, completed considerably less schooling than did the younger groups. For instance, only 17 percent of men and 3 percent of women age 60–64 had at least a secondary degree, compared with 56 percent of men and 75 percent of women age 25–29. Among these younger Qataris, 26 percent of men and 46 percent of women had completed post-secondary schooling.

Another pattern is the change in the relative schooling of men and women. Older Qatari men are better educated than older Qatari women, but this pattern is reversed for Qataris younger than 40. For instance, Qatari women age 25–29 are almost twice as likely as their male counterparts to have pursued post-secondary schooling (46 percent for women and 26 percent for men). And while the educational attainment of successive age groups of Qatari women has steadily improved,

[3]   The reason for reporting figures for persons age 25 and older is to focus on completed schooling levels.

it is not clear that this is true for the men. In fact, the percentage of men pursuing post-secondary studies declined sharply for the younger cohorts—42 percent of men age 40–44 pursued post-secondary education while only 26 percent of men age 25–29 did. The clear implication of these results is that the educational attainment is trending in opposite directions for men and women, with women becoming better educated over time while men's level of education declines.

Economy and Industry

Qatar is one of the world's wealthiest countries, and its economy has grown dramatically over the past few years. Recent data put Qatar's per capita income at $50,600, the highest rate among the GCC member states (Institute of International Finance, Inc., 2006) and a figure that would be even higher if expatriates were excluded from the calculation.

Oil and gas account for more than 60 percent of the gross domestic product, roughly 85 percent of export earnings, and 70 percent of government revenues (Central Intelligence Agency, 2007). In 2003, Qatar's average output of crude oil was 750,000 barrels per day (Qatar Ministry of Foreign Affairs, undated). Proven oil reserves should ensure continued output at current levels for approximately 23 years (Central Intelligence Agency, 2007).

The same year that Qatar became independent, vast natural gas reserves were discovered in northern Qatar. In the 1990s, Qatar began exploiting its offshore natural gas reserves in the North Field, one of the world's largest natural gas fields (U.S. Library of Congress, 1994). Qatar's proved reserves of natural gas exceed 25 trillion cubic meters, which is more than 5 percent of the world's total and the third largest reserve in the world (Central Intelligence Agency, 2007).

Before Qatar began exploiting its natural gas fields, its wealth depended heavily on oil revenues, making it vulnerable to fluctuations in the foreign market. Qatar's leaders have long recognized the need to develop industrial capabilities to reduce the country's dependence on oil revenue (Nafi, 1983). Revenues from crude oil exports have been used to fund a range of development projects within the country. In the 1970s, industries were developed in petrochemicals, chemical fertilizers, natural gas liquids, and steel. In 1974, the Qatar Steel Company Limited came into being after Qatar and two Japanese companies agreed to produce reinforcing steel bars for export. The Qatar National Cement Company had already been established in 1965 and had begun production in 1969. Both of these manufacturing enterprises were developed to produce exports, but they also provided building materials to support the intensive local construction efforts that began in the 1970s (Nafi, 1983). In addition, the government has encouraged and subsidized investment in medical services and tourism.

Qatar's economy is expected to continue to grow and diversify. However, this may have little effect on the post-secondary education choices of Qataris because of established employment practices and incentives.

Employment

As discussed earlier, non-Qataris make up the bulk of Qatar's population. Table 2.4 shows that they make up the bulk of the labor force as well: 84 percent, compared with 48 percent for Qataris.[4] The table also shows that Qataris are more likely than non-Qataris to be students (which accords with the fact that expatriates are predominantly in the country to work) and that Qatari men are more likely than Qatari women to be in the labor force. Nearly half of Qatari women are not in the labor force, a statistic reflective of a society in which women's traditional role is in the home.

Data from the Planning Council's 2001 survey of the labor force indicate an unemployment rate of around 12 percent: 22 percent of women, and 7 percent of men (Planning Council, 2002). Unemployment is concentrated among those seeking work for the first time, which means that young people are the group most at risk. The

---

[4]   The labor force is defined as those persons age 15 and over who are currently employed or are currently unemployed and actively looking for work.

Table 2.4

Labor Force Participation of Qataris and Non-Qataris Age 15 and Over, by Gender

	Percent		
	In Labor Force	With Student Status	Not in Labor Force
Qataris			
Males	68	20	12
Females	29	24	48
Total	48	22	30
Non-Qataris			
Males	95	4	1
Females	47	11	42
Total	84	5	11
All males	92	6	2
All females	41	15	44
Total	77	9	14

SOURCE: Planning Council, 2005.

unemployment rate for those previously employed is only 1 percent, the lowest rate in the Gulf Region for this group (Planning Council, 2005).

Qatar's four main employment sectors are as follows:

1. The government sector, which consists of ministries and other exclusively government institutions, such as the military and government councils.
2. State-owned enterprises, which are entities fully owned by the state. Some of these operate with independent budgets; others receive their budgets directly from the government. One example is Qatar Petroleum Corporation.
3. The mixed sector, which consists of establishments owned through a partnership between the government and a local national or foreign entity. One example of such an establishment is Qatar Airways, which is 50 percent state owned and 50 percent privately owned.

4.   The private sector, which comprises establishments privately owned and operated. In some industries, private enterprises must be at least 51 percent Qatari owned.[5]

Table 2.5 shows the distribution of Qatari employment by occupation and sector. As can be seen, Qataris make up only about 11 percent of the total workforce and are mainly employed in the government sector (about 77 percent of all employed Qataris are in this sector). One important trend that shows up here is that only about 4 percent of Qatari workers were employed in the private sector in 2004, and this number was down from 10 percent in 1998. Furthermore, only 2 percent of Qataris were self-employed or ran businesses in 2004, down from 6 percent in the mid-1980s (Planning Council, 2005). Non-Qataris make up the bulk of the labor market in all sectors and constitute 99 percent of the private sector, which employs three-quarters of

Table 2.5
Qatari Employment, by Occupation and Sector, 2004

| | Percent in Sector | | | | |
Occupation	Govt.	Govt. Enterprise	Mixed	Private	All
Senior official, manager	5	1	0	2	8
Professional	22	3	1	0	26
Technician	11	3	1	0	16
Clerk	16	4	1	1	22
Sales and service worker	8	1	0	1	10
Craftsman	0	0	0	0	0
Plant operator	1	1	0	0	2
Elementary worker	2	1	0	0	3
Total number of Qataris	38,936	6,661	2,457	2,228	50,282
% of all Qatari workers	77	13	5	4	100
% of all workers	50	27	20	1	11

SOURCE: Planning Council, 2005, Table 2.10.

---

[5]   The industries in which private enterprises must be 51 percent owned by Qataris are agriculture, tourism, health services, education services, oil- and gas-related services, wholesale and retail trade, and finance. Also falling under this rule are enterprises acting as agents for foreign companies (Planning Council, 2005).

the labor force and is the focus of diversification and expansion. What is evident from the data is that Qataris and non-Qataris essentially work in different labor markets.

Qataris and non-Qataris also work in different industries. Table 2.6 shows that Qataris tend not to work in agriculture, fishing, construction, trade, tourism, and domestic services. Rather, their employment is concentrated in public administration and defense and in education. Qatari women who work outside the home have traditionally been employed as teachers, nurses, and clerks. Gender segregation in the workplace is still common in education and government workplaces, but there is much less gender segregation in private workplaces.

Qataris have historically found employment in the government sector to be more attractive than employment in the private sector for several reasons. Qataris prefer not to work in jobs that involve manual labor; when they work in the private sector, they almost always do so in a managerial capacity (Winckler, 2000). The government jobs also provide greater total compensation—Qataris are paid a salary based on their level of education and are provided with benefits (e.g., interest-free mortgages to build houses on government-provided land, retirement pensions). In addition, Qataris are guaranteed that there will be a job for them in a government ministry when they graduate from secondary school or university. If they lose their government job, they continue to receive their salary and benefits until a comparable government job is found. Government offices have shorter working hours than other establishments and are generally open from 8 a.m. until 1 p.m. Government positions have historically also garnered more prestige than comparable jobs in the private sector, and the competition inherent to the private sector is absent in the government workplace. A common sentiment among employers in the private sector is that expatriates simply are better educated and trained (Gause, 1994) and are willing to work for lower wages.

The results of a survey of unemployed Qataris confirm the existence of a bias against private-sector work. For example, among the reasons cited by Qatari men for not accepting a job in the private or mixed sector were low wages (50 percent), undesirable hours of work (31 percent), and low social status (19 percent). Women cited their con-

Table 2.6
Employment, by Industry, 2004

Industry	Percent in Industry								
	Females			Males			Overall		
	Qatari	Other	All	Qatari	Other	All	Qatari	Other	All
Construction	0	1	1	1	34	31	1	30	27
Wholesale and retail trade	0	4	3	2	15	14	1	14	12
Domestic services	0	60	46	0	7	6	0	14	12
Public administration and defense	29	4	10	66	7	13	55	7	12
Manufacturing	0	1	1	2	12	11	1	10	9
Education	53	9	19	5	2	2	19	3	5
Mining and quarrying	2	2	2	10	4	5	8	4	4
Transport, storage, communications	1	4	3	2	4	3	2	4	3
Real estate, renting, business	0	1	1	1	3	3	1	3	3
Health and social work	9	10	10	2	1	1	4	2	3
Hotels and restaurants	0	1	1	0	3	3	0	3	2
Agriculture, hunting, forestry	0	0	0	0	3	3	0	3	2
Other commercial, social, personal	1	2	2	3	2	2	3	2	2
Financial intermediation	2	2	2	1	1	1	2	1	1
Electricity, gas, water	1	0	0	4	1	1	3	1	1
Fishing	0	0	0	0	1	0	0	0	0
Totals (absolute numbers)	15,163	49,295	64,458	35,119	337,984	373,103	50,282	387,279	437,561

SOURCE: Planning Council, 2005, Table 2.12.
NOTE: Percentages subject to rounding errors.

cern about working in a mixed-gender environment (76 percent), low social status (53 percent), and, to a far lesser extent, low wages (18 percent) (Planning Council, 2002).

The government has initiated several "Qatarization" programs to increase the number of Qataris in the workforce. According to Qatari Labor Law No. 3 of 1962, a vacant position in the workforce must be offered to a Qatari before it is offered to anyone else. If no Qatari takes the position, it can be offered to a non-Qatari Arab and then to a non-Arab foreigner (Article 10, as reported in Winckler, 2000). In the early 1970s, a decision was made to Qatarize administrative posts in the government sector; by the 1990s, 96 percent of the top school-administrative positions were held by Qataris. In May 1997, the Emir decreed that private-sector businesses must ensure that at least 20 percent of their employees are Qataris (Winckler, 2000). According to an industry-wide Strategic Qatarization Plan, the Qatarization target for the energy industry was a 50 percent national workforce by the end of 2005. This plan went into effect on June 1, 2000, and is the most comprehensive Qatarization plan in the state's history. Employers now compete for Qataris who have developed specific skills in high-demand fields, such as engineering and finance. However, a recent analysis indicates that Qatarization policies aimed at boosting the national workforce are not working, partly because of the education system's limited ability to produce Qataris trained for high-productivity jobs (Planning Council, 2005).

Summary

Qatar's leadership envisions moving the nation toward a 21st century knowledge society in which citizens participate fully in the economy and society. Other goals are to streamline the public sector, diversify the economy to develop other industries, and generally expand the private sector (Planning Council, 2005). The leadership realizes that education is crucial to realizing what it envisions, and has made great strides in bringing about the reform of the K–12 education sector and expanding opportunities for quality post-secondary education in Qatar and abroad.

However, as outlined in this chapter, there are a number of evident barriers, the most noteworthy being

- The K–12 education system is weak, and students are not adequately prepared for post-secondary education. The effects of the K–12 set of reforms currently under way will take a long time to manifest themselves. At the post-secondary level, Qatar University is embarking on its own set of reforms, and the Education City campuses are a relatively new venture.
- Qatari nationals make up only 11 percent of the total labor force, making Qatar highly dependent on a growing expatriate workforce to fill the many managerial and professional positions outside of the government sector and to populate nearly all jobs in the private sector.
- Qataris prefer to work in the public rather than the private sector, especially in government jobs, which provide higher salaries and benefits, shorter working hours, job security, and protection from competition with expatriates better qualified than they are.
- Qatari women are higher academic achievers than are Qatari men, but are less likely to pursue career employment. Most Qatari women work in the education profession. Qatari men lack the qualifications to replace non-nationals in high-skilled, high-demand occupations and yet have high expectations of being employed in well-paying, secure jobs.
- Qatarization policies to re-direct Qatari participation in the labor force are not working as well as intended. For example, the number of Qataris who can work in the private sector is still limited by Qataris' lack of qualifications and willingness.

It is essential that as the Qatari leadership considers how to broaden and expand post-secondary education, especially in key areas of economic expansion, it take into account the fact that historical preferences for certain types of employment and labor market policies create strong incentives to maintain the status quo.

CHAPTER THREE

Skill and Occupational Demands

Qatar's economic development and social development together present many opportunities for Qataris to assume important roles in society. Because of the relatively small number of Qataris—the indigenous population is estimated to be about one-fourth of the state's 850,000 residents—it is especially important to identify the career fields and skills that are in demand now and will be in demand in the future. We considered the needs of employers, the preferences of young people, and independent research on Qatar's future economic and social development in order to identify skills, career fields, and occupational levels likely to be in highest demand. We saw this as a first step toward determining whether Qatar's current post-secondary offerings are adequate or new investments will be needed.

This chapter addresses the demand for skills and occupations in Qatar and the education and training needed to meet that demand. First, we describe the demand in the Qatar economy as a whole and summarize the employment patterns for Qataris using the most-recent data available (Planning Council, 2005). We then present data from the employer interviews we conducted in a discussion of employers' skill needs. Next, we outline the levels of education and training that might be needed to create the skills that are in demand. We then turn to the types of jobs that young Qataris are engaged in or aspire to have, using data from our surveys of young people who graduated from secondary school in 1998 and secondary school seniors. Our question here is, Do their patterns of education and employment—or their aspirations for education and employment—reflect current and future demand?

Current and Future Needs

The Planning Council's 2005 report, which used 2004 census data for Qatar, adopted a Qatar-specific instrument, the Manpower Requirements Simulation Model (MRSM), to identify recent trends in employment and education changes and to offer insights into what the future will be like if recent trends persist.[1] Early application of the MRSM indicated that, based on recent trends, most of the increased employment for Qatari males will be in the professional, technician, and sales and service worker occupations.[2] Much of this increase has been in the government sector, mainly in public administration, but with some gains in government enterprises. For Qatari females, the pattern is similar. The employment of Qatari female clerks in public administration has increased substantially, but substantial increases are also evident in professional jobs for females in the government sector, evenly divided between public administration and education.

A forecast of future employment growth (Planning Council, 2005) based on "hot spots"—promising employment opportunities for Qataris—suggested that:

- For Qatari men, the prime source of employment for new entrants into the labor market will be in public administration, the oil and gas industry, and the electricity, gas, and water utilities.[3] Qataris will continue the trend of replacing non-Qataris in existing jobs, provided that they acquire the necessary education and skills.

---

[1]   The Planning Council (2005) report notes that the MRSM is already in need of an update and has some data limitations and deficiencies that weaken the accuracy of forecasts, in some cases by 20 percent. The Planning Council is expanding the model to include estimates for more-detailed occupational classifications.

[2]   The Planning Council's analysis used the International Standard Classification of Occupations 88 (ISCO-88) occupational codes. For example, "professional" includes teachers, architects, and scientists, whereas "sales and service" includes hairdressers, police, and childcare workers. Additional information can be found in Elias and Birch, 1994, and on the International Labour Organization's ISCO-88 Web site: http://www.ilo.org/public/english/bureau/stat/isco/isco88/index.htm.

[3]   This analysis incorporates only very broad occupational categories and is based on growth of Qatari and non-Qatari employment between 1997 and 2004.

- Qatari women have prospered in public administration and as clerks in many industries, and there is scope for them to continue to do so. They will also benefit from growth in the education and health sectors; they have been successful in securing jobs as teachers and school administrators.
- Although the private sector is growing rapidly, it does not appear to be a fertile source of desirable employment opportunities for Qatari men and women. The reason for this, as discussed in Chapter Two, is that Qataris are not attracted to or are not qualified for the available jobs. Similarly, although Qatar is promoting the tourism and hospitality industry, Qataris show a lack of interest in working in this sector.

The formal employer interviews undertaken in this study provided more-specific information about occupational and skill needs. Table 3.1 identifies the occupational needs that employers mentioned, organized by the main occupational categories of the ISCO-88.[4] The data vary quite a lot in terms of specific jobs within these broad occupational categories. For example, Qatar Petroleum needs technicians and engineers, while the Hamad Medical Corporation needs medical professionals, especially doctors and nurses.

Most of the occupations mentioned as being in demand are in mid-level or higher positions in specific technical areas. Only two employers, both government organizations, said they have a need for more clerical workers. Except for the Qatar Armed Forces, all employers said they have difficulty finding qualified candidates for high-demand occupations.

A few occupations appear to be in demand across two or more organizations: information and communication technology (ICT) specialists, administrators and managers, engineers, customer service representatives, security specialists, and finance. If we include the informal interviews we conducted in our tally, engineering and administrator/

---

[4] Responses that could not be classified are shown as "other." The Ministry of Civil Service Affairs and Housing (MoCSAH) is not included in Table 3.1 because the interviewees did not provide information on occupational demands.

Table 3.1
Occupational Needs Mentioned by Employers

Need	Qatar Airways	Qatar Armed Forces	Supreme Council for Information and Technology	Ministry of Interior	SEC Evaluation Institute	Qatar Petroleum	Qatar National Bank	Hamad Medical Corporation	Sheraton Hotel Doha	SEC Education Institute
Professional occupations										
School support specialist										√
Curriculum specialist										√
School evaluation specialist					√					
Student assessment specialist					√					
Teacher										√
IT specialist			√				√	√		
Engineer						√		√		
Physician								√		
Ph.D. researcher					√					
Human resources professional	√									
Nurse								√		
Technicians and associate professionals										
Technician						√				
Finance	√								√	
Marketing	√									
Security						√			√	
Administrator/manager	√	√	√	√		√	√	√		
Clerks										
Clerk/secretary				√	√					
Sales and service workers										
Sales									√	
Customer service rep							√		√	
Bank teller							√			
Hostess									√	
Other										√
Specialist and expert (unspecified)			√							√

manager are the unfilled occupations mentioned most often. Overall, the interview data align with the Planning Council study in pointing to demand in the "professional" and "technician and associate professional" occupational categories and, specifically for women, in the "clerical" occupations.

We also asked employers about specific skill needs. Following the broader literature on skills (e.g., Secretary's Commission on Achieving Necessary Skills, 1991; Stasz, 2001; Stasz et al., 1996), we viewed skills as falling within four broad categories:

1. Academic, or "cognitive," skills. These are generally associated with subject-matter areas defined by the various school disciplines, such as English, Arabic, history, and science. Knowledge about these subjects is primarily gained in school and is expected to be broadly transferable to situations and circumstances outside of school.

2. General, or "generic," skills. These include critical thinking skills, communication skills, and teamwork skills. Like the academic skills, they are thought to be broadly transferable across work settings, although they can take on different meanings in different work contexts.[5]

3. Technical skills. These are specific skills needed in a particular occupation and may include references to academic skills (e.g., the statistical knowledge needed by researchers), or to knowledge of certain tools or processes (e.g., such as ICT skills).

4. Work-related attitudes or dispositions. These "soft skills" are perhaps the most difficult to define, because there is no accepted way to conceptualize them. They often refer to such personal characteristics as working hard, showing initiative, and taking responsibility.

Table 3.2 depicts the skills that employers mentioned within these four broad categories. The results indicate a high demand for English

---

[5]   Problem solving, for example, is a general term that represents a particular competency, but the process itself varies with different tasks or situations (Stasz, 2001).

Table 3.2

Skill Demands Mentioned by Employers

Skill	Qatar Airways	Qatar Armed Forces	Supreme Council for Information and Technology	Ministry of Interior	SEC Evaluation Institute	Qatar Petroleum	MoCSAH	Qatar National Bank	Hamad Medical Corporation	Sheraton Hotel Doha	SEC Education Institute
Academic											
English	√		√	√	√	√		√	√	√	
Math skills						√		√			
Science skills	√					√			√		
Generic											
Communication				√	√			√			
Teamwork skills	√				√						
Creativity			√	√							
Analytic/critical thinking	√			√	√						
Technical											
Student assessment					√						
Computer skills			√	√				√	√		
Knowledge of ICT sector			√	√					√		
Research skills				√	√						
Marketing	√							√			
Business/management	√		√					√			
Finance/accounting	√							√			
Customer service skills								√		√	
Technical skills (unspecified)	√		√			√			√		
Security professional skills				√		√					
Curriculum design										√	√
School support											√
Attitudes and dispositions											
Interpersonal skills								√		√	
Loyalty/commitment								√	√		
Work habits								√			
Good attitude	√	√	√	√	√	√	√	√			
Willingness to learn			√			√		√	√		
Hard working								√			

language skills, in both the private and the broader government sector. They also indicate that two or more employers needed people with basic mathematics and science skills, and two or more were looking for applicants with communication skills, teamwork skills, and creativity. Of the technical, specialized skills needed, ICT-related skills were the most mentioned, followed by critical thinking/analytic skills, business administration and management skills, and clerical skills. At least two organizations mentioned skill needs in research, marketing, finance/accounting, and security. Not surprisingly, nearly all of the organizations indicated that they value employees who have a good work attitude, and three mentioned a willingness to learn as important. Two indicated that loyalty to the company and commitment are needed.

By and large, the employers we interviewed were not satisfied with the quality of skills possessed by Qatari secondary school and university graduates. Most employers viewed Qatari graduates' English skills as poor, and about half complained about poor communication skills. Poor technical skills were also frequently mentioned.

Employers noted that Qatari graduates had poor work attitudes as well, and some specifically mentioned lack of loyalty or commitment to the company. Loyalty was particularly an issue for employers that had invested in employee training and then had the employees leave for organizations offering better pay and benefits.[6] It was also an issue for employers working toward Qatarization targets, since any Qatari leaving the organization would be a setback.[7] At least one organization, however, claimed that employees who left for better positions were not a problem—it saw itself as contributing to the skills of the country's citizens no matter where those citizens worked.

According to the employers, the work attitudes of Qataris and non-Qataris differ. Employers mentioned that Qatari employees exhibited an unwillingness to work in shifts (especially on evening shifts) or

---

[6] Employers and employees, of course, may have different values with respect to "soft skills." From the employee's perspective, for example, leaving a company for a better position elsewhere may simply be a rational career choice.

[7] As discussed in Chapter Two, Qatarization refers to a set of labor-market policies and programs for increasing the employment of nationals and regulating the use of expatriate workers.

outside Doha, as well as lack of enthusiasm or motivation for the job. In addition, Qataris expected to be given a management or supervisory position regardless of their experience or qualifications. One interviewee noted that Qatari men were sometimes unwilling to work for female supervisors. And two noted that Qataris tended toward shyness, which sometimes made them reluctant to work in jobs dealing with the public.

Implications for Education and Training

The results from the Planning Council research and from our employer interviews suggest that there will be a high demand for university graduates for jobs in the professional category (e.g., teachers, physicians, positions related to specialized education) and for many jobs in the technician and associate professional category (e.g., marketing, finance, business administration). Other jobs, such as secretarial positions, security workers, or hostesses, can be filled by secondary school graduates or individuals with post-secondary diplomas or technical qualifications. In many cases, these technical qualifications will be earned as part of employer-sponsored training (such as are offered by Qatar Petroleum or Hamad Medical Corporation).

The broad demand for English and ICT skills suggests that these skills need to be provided either as part of the core curriculum in schools and at university or by organizations that specialize in teaching them. The K–12 education reform currently under way in Qatar emphasizes English language learning and incorporates new curriculum standards and assessments for it. Use of ICT in schools is also growing, especially in the new, Independent schools (Brewer et al., 2007).

Generic skills, such as critical thinking/analytic skills could also be advanced in schools. Both the curriculum reform currently under way in secondary schools and the new core curriculum that is to be established at Qatar University are designed to enhance these types of skills (Qatar University, 2006).

Improving the soft skills—i.e., attitudes and disposition toward work—within Qatar's traditional education system may prove to be the most difficult of the tasks in this area, however. Research suggests that it is possible to teach positive work-related skills and attitudes within a secondary school curriculum, but new curriculum or program designs and specialized teacher training would be needed first (e.g., Stasz et al., 1993).

Some "soft" skills, such as loyalty to an employer or being motivated at work, may be individual characteristics or behaviors that are difficult to change through an educational intervention. As discussed in Chapter Two, most Qataris work in the government sector, where current employment policies provide good benefits, job security, and no performance-based rewards or penalties. In these circumstances, there is little reason for employees to work hard, show initiative, or even take their work seriously. As noted in the previous section, some employers we interviewed complained that lack of motivation or enthusiasm is endemic among Qataris, particularly among Qatari men. Changes in employment policies and practices may be needed if the motivational and attitudinal problems that concern many employers and ultimately affect productivity and performance are to be mitigated.

Employers in this study echoed other research (Brewer et al., 2007) in noting shortcomings in the skills of both secondary school and university graduates. Two employers, however—the Qatar Armed Forces and the Sheraton Hotel Doha—were generally satisfied with the basic skills of secondary school graduates.

It is not unusual to find that employers in Qatar are dissatisfied with the skills of graduates—the same result can be found in studies of employers in many other countries. One common strategy for raising employer satisfaction and increasing the likelihood that graduates will be prepared for work is to forge formal relationships between education institutions and employers. These can take different forms, such as employer representation on advisory boards, input into curriculum development, and sponsorship of interns or work schemes (e.g., Bailey, Hughes, and Moore, 2004; Organisation for Economic Co-Operation and Development, 2000).

Some Qatari employers, like those in other countries, have direct links with the education system; Qatar Petroleum, for example, has connections with the College of the North Atlantic and with Qatar

University through an advisory board and sponsorship of students. Data from providers of post-secondary education, however, indicate that several of them have no formal relationships with employers. Recent studies conclude that with notable exceptions (e.g., Qatar Petroleum), overall links between education and the labor market are weak (Planning Council, 2005; Brewer et al., 2007). Even if individual relationships between employers and education institutions were more widespread, Qatar presently has no mechanism for producing the coordination among labor and education planning authorities that is essential for joint guidance of workforce development (Planning Council, 2005).

Whether they are satisfied with graduates' skills or not, nearly all organizations in our study have invested in formal and informal training, and this training has been quite extensive in several cases.[8] Because most Qataris work in the public sector, an issue of importance for Qatar is the cost of this training. Qatar provides free education to citizens up through university level. Unlike other countries, Qatar also supports further job-related training in its large government and public enterprise sectors. In other countries, it is typical for employers or individuals to bear some or all of these job-related training costs.

In sum, like many other countries, Qatar recognizes the key relationship between education and economic development, and is aiming to increase educational opportunities for its citizens. We have so far identified some occupational and skill demands, a few of which are well recognized and can be met through educational intervention. Chapter Five examines the question of whether the current set of post-secondary institutions or opportunities is sufficient for meeting demands. However, the supply of skills also depends on Qataris' education and occupational choices, which is the issue we turn to next.

_____

[8]   For example, at Qatar Petroleum, a graduate of Qatar University's engineering program can expect to receive up to six more years of structured training and work experience before becoming fully qualified.

Patterns of Education and Employment

The data from our study provide two important perspectives on patterns of education and employment—that of young people who graduated from secondary school in 1998, and that of 18-year-old secondary school seniors set to graduate in 2006. The data from the 1998 group illuminate the transition from secondary school to higher education and work; the 2006 group's data reveal seniors' education and employment aspirations. These data allowed us to determine whether recent choices and future aspirations generally align with economic demand, but they did not provide robust estimates about over- or under-supply. However, our survey data supplemented available census information by providing insights into the reasons behind education and employment choices and aspirations. Understanding what individuals value when making decisions about education and work can help policymakers craft the incentives that will be effective in increasing educational pursuits toward high-demand occupations. This section looks at transitions and expected transitions for our two groups overall. Chapter Four focuses further on those individuals who neither pursue nor plan to pursue post-secondary education, because this group is of particular concern to policymakers.

What Do Young Qataris Do After Secondary School?

Patterns of Post-Secondary Education. Our survey of Qataris who graduated from secondary school in 1998 indicates that most young people in this group, or cohort, pursued some type of post-secondary education: two-thirds acquired some post-secondary education and over half attained a university degree. Women were much more likely than men to pursue their education beyond secondary school, including earning a university degree—79 percent of the women in the sample had some post-secondary education, compared with 52 percent of the men (p < .01), and over 70 percent of the women earned a university degree, compared with only 30 percent of the men (p < .01). These results are in line with the census data reported in Chapter Two, which demonstrate that women pursue more education than men do overall.

Decisions about pursuing post-secondary education and following particular courses of study have important implications for the labor market because they affect the types of skills held by the college-educated segment of the labor force. Figure 3.1 shows the fields of study for those individuals in the 1998 cohort who sought post-secondary education (35 men and 39 women, equivalent to 79 percent of the total sample).

Of the males who sought post-secondary schooling (N = 35), 40 percent studied computers or engineering, and about 23 percent studied either business or law. Of the males in the "other" category, 23 percent went into military-related fields and some technical areas (e.g., process technician).

The females in the 1998 cohort who pursued a post-secondary education (N = 39) were more likely than the males to go into the humanities and arts and education. In fact, no male reported that he studied education, even though the field is open to men.

Figure 3.1
Fields of Study Pursued in Post-Secondary Education, 1998 Cohort

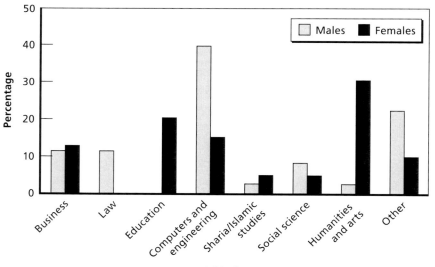

However, about 15 percent of the women studied computers and engineering, and about 13 percent studied business.

What men and women choose to study at the post-secondary level has important implications. As previously discussed, employers are looking for employees with specific skills, and there is a direct connection between the field of study that a post-secondary student pursues and the types of skills that person brings to the labor market. For example, many employers expressed a desire for university graduates with technical skills, which means there is a need for more graduates in engineering, mathematics, science, ICT, and the like. Although 40 percent of the men in the cohort who went on to post-secondary schooling pursued computers or engineering, the proportion who fell into the "other" category was substantial. Women, who are more likely than men to pursue a post-secondary education, are most likely to earn degrees in education. These data suggest that, given employers' relatively high demand for technical skills, the deficit in these skills will remain unless more men earn college degrees in technical fields and/or more women switch their field of study to the technical field.

Patterns of Employment. When we looked at the patterns of employment for the cohort of 1998 graduates, we found that the majority of individuals were working for government ministries or in a government enterprise. As Table 3.3 shows, considerably more women than men were working in the ministries (72 percent compared with 49 percent; p = .06), whereas men's employment was more equally distributed between the ministries and government enterprises. Only 28 percent of the women were working in government enterprises, compared with 42 percent of men, although this difference is not statistically significant (p = .25).

Regardless of gender, very few individuals in this sample were working outside of the ministries or government enterprises. If the private sector is to play an increasingly important role in Qatar's economy, the lack of young Qataris willing to work in the private sector and possessing the skills to do so is a concern.

We asked those surveyed to report their most recent occupation and then categorized the results using occupational codes similar to

Table 3.3
Current Employment, 1998 Cohort, by Type of Organization and Gender

Type of Organization	Percent Currently Employed[a]		
	Female	Male	Overall
Government ministry	72	49	61
Govt.-owned company	28	42	35
Private company[b]	0	2	1
Other	0	7	3
Sample size	25	43	68

[a] Weighted to reflect proportion of men and women in the population for the 1998 cohort.

[b] Includes private charitable organizations and private businesses, family owned or otherwise.

those used in the recent Planning Council study.[9] Table 3.4 shows the results. As can be seen, a fifth of the men in the sample reported their most recent job as a professional occupation, and 18 percent had most recently worked in the military or police. About 15 percent reported their most recent job as clerk or associate professional (e.g., legal researcher, inspector). Only 9 percent indicated technician or operator.

Some of the jobs held by men were not held by any women in this sample (e.g., being in the military or police). The highest percentage of women in this cohort (44 percent) reported that their most recent job was as a teacher, a job reported by only 4 percent of the men (p < .01). Gender differences for the other occupational categories were smaller. Women were more likely than men to work as clerks and a little less likely than men to hold jobs in the professional occupations. The percentages of women and men working as associate professionals were similar, 11 percent for women and 13 percent for men.

To help understand why the 1998 graduates pursued the level of education they did, we asked them the level of education needed for their most recent occupation. Fifty percent of the women and 28 percent of the men responded that their job required a university degree

---

[9]   We used the ISCO-88 classification scheme (details of the coding are provided in Appendix A). Although ISCO-88 categorizes police as service workers, we chose to combine police with the military because these occupations are government positions found attractive by Qatari men who do not want to pursue post-secondary schooling.

Table 3.4
Most Recent Job Held, 1998 Cohort, by Gender

Most Recent Job	Percent Holding Job		
	Female	Male	Overall
Associate professional	11	13	12
Clerk	19	16	17
Elementary worker	0	4	2
Legislator/senior officer	4	4	4
Military/police	0	18	9
Operator	0	9	4
Professional	15	20	17
Service worker	0	2	1
Teacher	44	4	25
Technician	7	9	8
Sample size	27	45	72

NOTE: Rounding prevents columns from totaling 100 percent.

$(p = .06)$. This disparity partly stems from the large percentage of women who go into teaching. Over 60 percent of women with a university degree listed teacher as their most recent job. In contrast, 14 percent of women and 42 percent of men indicated that they worked in jobs requiring only a secondary school diploma $(p < .01)$.

Job Characteristics That Matter. Earlier we noted possible mismatches between the pattern of employment among Qataris who graduated in 1998 and labor market demands. These graduates overwhelmingly are working in government ministries and government enterprises, and government policy and labor market forecasts indicate that more Qataris should be working in the private sector. An understanding of the reasons behind this mismatch may help policymakers develop incentives for individuals to make choices that better align with labor market needs. To gather information on these reasons, we asked those members of the 1998 cohort who were or had been employed to rate how important a number of job characteristics (e.g., salary, benefits, challenge of work) had been to their choice of job/career. Table 3.5 shows the results.

According to both the men and the women, the most important job characteristic is making one feel respected and appreciated, followed by job security and opportunities for career advancement. Both

Table 3.5
Importance of Job Characteristics to Choice of Job or Career, 1998 Cohort, by Gender

Characteristic	Means (Rank Order)[a]		
	Female	Male	Overall
Makes me feel respected and appreciated	3.82 (1)	3.77 (1)	3.79 (1)
Job security	3.68 (2)	3.53 (4)	3.61 (2)
Opportunities for career advancement	3.32 (6)	3.72 (2)	3.51 (3)
Opportunity to contribute to society	3.43 (3)	3.53 (5)	3.48 (4)
Opportunity to get more training	3.39 (5)	3.55 (3)	3.47 (5)
Friendly colleagues	3.43 (4)	3.30 (11)	3.37 (6)
Allows time to be with family	3.11 (9)	3.37 (9)	3.23 (7)
Interesting work	3.18 (8)	3.26 (12)	3.22 (8)
Challenging work	3.04 (10)	3.17 (13)	3.10 (9)
Salary	2.71 (15)	3.43 (7)	3.06 (10)
Vacations	3.25 (7)	2.81 (16)	3.04 (11)
Retirement benefits	2.62 (17)	3.37 (8)	2.99 (12)
Other benefits	2.64 (16)	3.34 (10)	2.98 (13)
Housing benefits	2.48 (18)	3.47 (6)	2.96 (14)
Prestige	2.93 (12)	2.85 (15)	2.89 (15)
Not expected to work long hours	2.96 (11)	2.74 (17)	2.86 (16)
Bonuses	2.82 (14)	2.89 (14)	2.85 (17)
Women-only work environment	2.86 (13)	1.84 (18)	2.39 (18)
Mixed-gender work environment	1.39 (19)	1.42 (19)	1.41 (19)
Sample size[b]	28	47	75

[a] Respondents rated each characteristic as follows: 1, not important; 2, somewhat important; 3, very important; 4, extremely important; 0, don't know. Scores were calculated as means after dropping all "don't know" (0) responses.
[b] Varies slightly across questions.

genders assigned salary and other monetary benefits middle ranking and considered working in a mixed-gender environment unimportant.

However, the importance of a number of job characteristics was viewed differently by men and women. Not surprisingly, the difference in the average importance of a single-gender work environment was sizable, with about 68 percent of the women reporting that a single-gender environment is very important or extremely important, compared with only about 25 percent of the men (p < .01). Women saw vacations as more important than men did (p < .04). In contrast, men saw job compensation in the form of salary and various types of benefits as more important (p < .01).

These results suggest that policies aimed at creating incentives for Qataris to pursue particular types of jobs may need to differ for men and women. They may also help explain why Qataris are attracted to certain types of jobs or organizations. For example, job security was ranked highly by both men and women, and government-related positions are more apt to guarantee job security than are private companies. A job that allows one time to be with family was also highly rated, and government jobs generally have shorter working hours than do jobs in the private sector (Planning Council, 2005).

Interestingly, these data in some ways contradict the opinions expressed by employers and others we interviewed. Their prevailing opinion was that Qatari workers are mainly motivated by high salaries and benefits. However, monetary compensation was only one of a number of important job considerations for men in this 1998 cohort, and salary and benefits were deemed less important than many other characteristics by the women.

What Do Secondary School Seniors Aspire to?

We now turn from the secondary school graduates to secondary school seniors—a sample of 18-year-olds (N = 260) leaving secondary school in 2006 who were making decisions about their future education and employment. First, we asked these students to tell us what influenced their decisions about what do after graduating from secondary school, factors such as advice from parents and the availability of scholarships and jobs. Table 3.6 shows the results. As can be seen, for both genders, the factors cited as most important in making post-secondary plans were parental advice and religious beliefs: Advice from a parent was considered very or extremely important by 98 percent of students, and religious beliefs were cited by 96 percent. These factors were more important on average than personal interests, kinds of jobs open to the student, and societal expectations. The two least important factors cited were advice from friends and other family members.

Table 3.6
Factors Affecting Post-Secondary Plans, 2006 Cohort, by Gender

Factor	Means (Rank Order)[a]		
	Female	Male	Overall
Personal interests	3.47 (3)	3.34 (4)	3.41 (4)
Advice from father or mother	3.58 (2)	3.79 (1)	3.68 (2)
Advice from other family members	2.67 (8)	2.81 (8)	2.74 (8)
Advice from friends	2.47 (9)	2.49 (9)	2.48 (9)
Religious beliefs	3.78 (1)	3.74 (2)	3.76 (1)
Societal expectations	3.11 (5)	3.18 (6)	3.14 (5)
Enjoyment of learning and school	2.98 (7)	2.88 (7)	2.93 (7)
Kinds of jobs that are open to you	3.45 (4)	3.48 (3)	3.47 (3)
Whether you get a scholarship	2.98 (6)	3.20 (5)	3.09 (6)
Sample size[b]	151	103	254

[a] Respondents rated each characteristic as follows: 1, not important; 2, somewhat important; 3, very important; 4, extremely important; 0, don't know. Scores were calculated as means after dropping all don't know (0) responses.
[b] Varies slightly across questions.

Post-Secondary Educational Aspirations. Most of the female seniors (60 percent) were planning to attend university after graduating from high school; for the male seniors, the figure was smaller (37 percent) (p < 01). A small percentage of both males and females wanted to attend technical college after high school; about 49 percent of the males and 15 percent of the females indicated that they would go to work right after graduating. Some students were unsure of their post-graduation plans (7 percent males, 14 percent females), and about 1 percent of the female seniors said they would remain at home. These data indicate that the trend for Qatari females to pursue post-secondary education in greater numbers than Qatari men is likely to continue.

However, when the seniors were asked about the preparation they would need to get their desired job, about 51 percent of both the males and females reported that they would need a university degree (either in Qatar or abroad), and an additional 8 percent reported that they would need further training. These data do not completely coincide with the post-secondary education plans, particularly for the male seniors. It may be that the males were aware that post-secondary education was necessary for their future careers but were not planning to pursue that education right after high school. They may also have been aware that obtaining a job in a government enterprise would lead to further education and training, since many jobs include formal course work at a technical college. Employers also support post-secondary study for promising employees.

Career Aspirations. We asked these students to indicate both the type of organization they would like to work in and the kind of job they would most like to have. Table 3.7 shows the results for where they would like to work. As can be seen, most of the students indicated government or government enterprise organizations. Males overwhelmingly selected the government as their main choice; females showed more interest than males in working in private charitable or religious organizations (18 percent versus 1 percent) and private companies (6 percent versus 1 percent) (p < .01).

As we had done with the cohort of 1998 post-secondary graduates, we asked this cohort of students to write in the type of job they would most like to have and coded their responses. Table 3.8 shows the results, which cover only a fraction of the cohort because nearly three-fourths of the seniors reported that they were unsure about their future career. Of those who provided countable responses to the question (N = 80), two-thirds of the males indicated that they aspired to join the military or police, and 21 percent of the females indicated that they aspired to be teachers (p < .01). Both genders indicated very low interest in clerical or service worker occupations; females showed more interest in professional or managerial jobs (e.g., legislator, senior officer,

Table 3.7
Desired Type of Employer, 2006 Cohort, by Gender

Type of Employer	Percent		
	Female	Male	Overall
Government ministry	33	75	54
Government-owned company	27	20	24
Private charity/religious organization	18	1	10
Private company	6	1	3
Unsure	16	3	10
Sample size	133	96	229

Table 3.8
Desired Occupation, 2006 Cohort, by Gender

Occupation	Percent		
	Female	Male	Overall
Associate professional	6	7	7
Clerk	3	0	2
Engineer	11	4	8
Legislator/senior officer/manager	23	9	16
Military/police	1	65	33
Professional	33	13	24
Service worker	3	0	2
Teacher	21	2	12
Sample size	45	35	80

chief executive officer). These data suggest that although many females aspire to be teachers—a traditional choice for women in Qatar—many others aspire to hold professional or managerial jobs.

Job Characteristics That Matter. Table 3.9 shows how the students in this cohort responded when asked to rate the importance of various job characteristics. As is evident, there was agreement among the students on the relative importance of several of these. Working in a mixed-gender workplace, prestige, having interesting work, and having a job that makes one feel respected and appreciated—all of these were considered important by males and females. Both genders also indicated that salary was important, although female students saw it as somewhat less so than male students ($p < .01$). Working in a women-only workplace (relevant for females only) was viewed as least important.

On the importance of other job characteristics, however, males and females tended to disagree. Male students were more concerned than female students about prestige ($p < .05$) and monetary benefits, such as bonuses, retirement benefits ($p < .05$), and other benefits (e.g., housing) ($p < .01$). Females rated friendly colleagues and not being expected to work long hours ($p < .01$) as more important than did males.

Some interesting differences between the views of these students and the members of the older cohort showed up with respect to the

Table 3.9
Importance of Job Characteristics to Choice of Job or Career, 2006 Cohort, by Gender

Characteristic	Mean (Rank Order)[a]		
	Female	Male	Overall
Makes me feel respected and appreciated	3.55 (3)	3.56 (4)	3.55 (3)
Job security	3.44 (6)	3.42 (6)	3.43 (6)
Opportunities for career advancement	3.22 (11)	3.08 (14)	3.15 (11)
Opportunity to contribute to society	3.27 (9)	3.29 (7)	3.28 (8)
Opportunity to get more training	3.22 (12)	3.11 (12)	3.16 (10)
Friendly colleagues	3.22 (10)	3.06 (15)	3.14 (12)
Allows time to be with family	3.17 (13)	3.22 (11)	3.20 (9)
Interesting work	3.54 (4)	3.48 (5)	3.51 (5)
Challenging work	3.46 (5)	3.28 (8)	3.37 (7)
Salary	3.37 (8)	3.70 (2)	3.53 (4)
Retirement benefits	2.67 (16)	3.10 (13)	2.88 (16)
Other benefits (e.g., housing)	2.75 (15)	3.24 (9)	2.99 (15)
Prestige	3.58 (2)	3.76 (1)	3.67 (2)
Not expected to work long hours	3.37 (7)	2.72 (17)	3.06 (14)
Bonuses	2.96 (14)	3.24 (10)	3.09 (13)
Women-only work environment	2.59 (17)	2.59 (18)	2.59 (18)
Health benefits	2.57 (18)	2.84 (16)	2.71 (17)
Mixed-gender work environment	3.71 (1)	3.67 (3)	3.69 (1)
Sample size[b]	151	103	254

[a] Respondents rated each characteristic as follows: 1, not important; 2, somewhat important; 3, very important; 4, extremely important; 0, don't know. Scores were calculated as means after dropping all don't know (0) responses.
[b] Varies slightly across questions.

working environment (see Table 3.5, above). For example, a women-only working environment was rated as less important by the younger females, who may be entering the labor force next year or in a few years' time, than by the older females: This characteristic was rated as very or extremely important by about half of the younger females, compared with 68 percent of the older females.[10] Working in a mixed-gender environment was rated highly by both males and females in the younger cohort (rank 3 and rank 1, respectively), whereas the older cohort rated it as least important. Relative to their elders, the younger cohort rated salary and prestige more highly but were much less concerned with opportunities for career advancement.

Finally, we asked the students to state whether they agreed or disagreed with a number of statements about school and work. Some of the statements—e.g., that private-sector jobs are harder than government jobs—were included to see whether students' views differed from those of employers and others we had interviewed. Table 3.10 shows the results.

The majority of the students appear to agree that a good education and good grades are important. A majority also appear to agree that good grades are helpful for getting a good job, although males were more likely to agree than were females ($p < .04$). The students seem to think that having a university degree makes a person more highly regarded but that it is not always necessary to go abroad to get the best university education.

Males and females have somewhat opposing views on women in the labor force. Ninety-four percent of females and only 53 percent of males agreed that women should be able to work outside the home ($p < .01$). Similarly, females were much more likely than males to agree that more jobs should be open to women ($p < .01$).

About three-fourths of students agreed or strongly agreed that the best jobs in Qatar are in the government, and 58 percent agreed that private-sector jobs are harder than government jobs. However, a fair percentage of students, about 20 percent, did not have an opinion about work in the private sector. Just over half of the students agreed with the statement that who you know is more important in getting a job than what you know.

---

[10] Any comparison of the two cohorts' female responses must be treated with caution. In surveying the 1998 cohort, this question was asked only of the women who were attached to the labor force. About one-third of the women were not employed at the time of the survey, so their views are not represented in the results.

Table 3.10
Views Toward School and Work by Gender, 2006 Cohort

Statement	Percent Agreeing or Strongly Agreeing with Statement		
	Female	Male	Overall
It is important to get a good education	95	95	95
Getting good grades at school helps you get a better job	90	97	93
You worry about getting a job that you will like	85	73	79
You have to go abroad to get the best education	43	54	48
People think better of you if you have a university degree	76	81	78
A job is not as important as the family	62	59	60
There should be more jobs open to women	94	63	79
The best jobs in Qatar are in the government (civil service)	71	78	74
People who study a technical field (e.g., engineering) can get a high-paying job	77	87	82
Work is harder in private companies than in government jobs	55	62	58
To get a good job, who you know is more important than what you know	57	54	55
Women should be able to work outside the home	94	53	74
Sample size[a]	151	103	254

[a] Varies slightly across questions.

Contrary to what we heard from employers and others we interviewed, these young Qataris reported that they are concerned about their grades and see good grades as an aid in getting a job. However, many of these students clearly feel that having connections also helps, and perhaps more than having qualifications.

Although a majority of the male students appear to feel that some prestige is attached to having a university degree and that studying in a technical field can lead to a higher paying job, only about 36 percent indicated that they were headed to university (see earlier discussion), and most of those who had decided on a career wanted to join the military or police. It appears that although most of the male students recognize that going to university is important—and employment trends point to the importance of university degrees—many decide early on to join the labor force without first attaining a post-secondary education. This suggests that males may be reading the labor market signals correctly, since they know they can find good government jobs requiring no more than a secondary degree. It may also mean that other factors are influencing these early choices. Chapter Four explores this issue further.

Summary and Key Findings

This chapter has addressed the demand for occupations and skills in Qatar, and the education and training needed to meet these demands. Overall, it appears that Qataris should prepare for professional and technical occupations, most of which require some post-secondary education or training. However, employment demands and patterns of education and employment are somewhat out of sync, especially for men. Qataris' preference for working in the government sectors remains strong.

Our key findings from this part of our analysis are as follows:

1. Employment demands for men will be in professional, technician, and sales and service worker occupations. The pattern is similar for women, except that they are also likely to find employment in clerical jobs and in professional jobs in the government.
2. Employers express high demand for skills in certain areas, especially English, ICT, and business. They also value the so-called soft skills, such as a good work attitude and a willingness to learn.
3. Patterns of employment for the 1998 secondary school graduates suggest that men are continuing to pursue careers in fields

other than those in demand, most notably in the military and police, and that large proportions of women still enter the teaching profession. A large proportion of graduates hold professional jobs, but whether they are doing so in sufficient numbers to meet current and future demands is unclear.

4. Occupational demand favors individuals with some post-secondary education supplemented by more-specific job training. Women are more likely to pursue post-secondary education than men.

5. The trend for Qatari women to pursue and achieve post-secondary education in greater numbers than Qatari men will likely continue given that twice as many females as males in our 2006 cohort planned to attend university or obtain a post-secondary diploma.

6. Similarly, the trend for Qataris to seek work in the government and government enterprises will also continue. Males overwhelmingly name the government as their main choice of employer, and most of the working women in our 1998 cohort (many of whom are teachers) are employed in a government ministry.

7. While women are more likely than men to pursue post-secondary education, they are still highly concentrated in such traditional occupations as teaching. Given that opportunities for women in the labor market appear to be expanding and that young females aspire to many types of careers, more may need to be done to tap this important human resource. Cultural expectations may still work against women's employment—e.g., the senior male and female students in the 2006 cohort had very different views about women working outside the home.

8. Secondary school students' choices for their future are highly influenced by parents and by religious beliefs. This suggests that appeals to parents and religious organizations (through, for instance, public relations campaigns) to encourage their children to pursue higher education and/or to highlight the need for professional and technical workers in Qatar may be one way to affect parental advice and students' choices.

CHAPTER FOUR

Qataris Who Do Not Pursue Post-Secondary Education

Young people who do not seek post-secondary education are of particular interest to policymakers in many nations, but this issue is especially important in Qatar for several reasons. First, as outlined in Chapter Three, occupational demand favors individuals who have a post-secondary education supplemented by more-specific job training. Second, census data and the survey results from our study point to a gender disparity in education—men are much less likely than women to pursue higher education—and this disparity appears to be increasing. Third, Qatari men currently have ample opportunities for employment in the government sector, even with only a secondary degree. The question thus becomes, How might more Qataris, especially men, be encouraged to pursue post-secondary studies related to high-demand occupations?

To shed light on this question, in this chapter we describe how we used survey data from the 1998 and 2006 cohorts (detailed in Chapter Three) to compare the characteristics and attitudes of and outcomes for Qataris who do and do not pursue a post-secondary education. The census data provide reliable population-wide information on educational attainment, but they offer information on neither the reasons behind educational choices nor the educational plans of students about to complete secondary school. Our comparisons can help isolate factors that may affect decisions about whether to pursue post-secondary education and, in doing so, may suggest ways in which policy can influence these decisions. In addition, the comparisons may suggest types

of post-secondary options that might attract students not currently following the post-secondary pathway.

Labor Market Outcomes for Those with Secondary and Post-Secondary Degrees

We first compared the labor market outcomes for individuals who went
on to post-secondary schooling and individuals who completed only
secondary school. We used two sources of information: published tables
from the 2004 census (Planning Council, 2004) and our survey of the
1998 secondary school graduates. In principle, census data should be
ideal for this analysis. However, the publicly available tabulations do
not report labor market outcomes separately by age and education. As
described in Chapter Two, older and younger Qataris have very different levels of schooling. Therefore, the overall relationship between
schooling and labor market performance may not accurately reflect this
relationship for younger Qataris. This limitation is important because
the experiences of younger Qataris are clearly the most relevant for
policymakers interested in addressing the needs of recent secondary
school graduates who do not pursue post-secondary schooling. Therefore, the results from the census are supplemented with evidence from
the survey of recent secondary school graduates.

Table 4.1 reports on the fraction of the 1998 cohort who were
not employed at the time of our survey. The results indicate that post-
secondary schooling is not strongly related to the probability of working: 37 percent of those with only a secondary degree were not employed,
compared with 34 percent of those with post-secondary degrees (p =
.76). For women, post-secondary schooling appears somewhat related
to the likelihood of working: 70 percent of women who pursued no
schooling beyond the secondary level were unemployed, compared
with 42 percent of women who pursued post-secondary schooling.
However, it should be borne in mind that the samples underlying this
comparison are quite small, and the difference is not statistically significant (p = .11). Among men, there is no evidence of a relationship
between post-secondary schooling and employment. Overall, these

Table 4.1
Unemployment, 1998 Cohort, by Level of Education and Gender

Unemployed	Percent with Education Level			
	Secondary	More Than Secondary	Overall	Sample Size
Whole cohort	37	34	35	97
Male	13	12	12	49
Female	70	42	48	48
Labor force[a]	18	23	21	83
Male	9	8	9	47
Female	40	29	31	36

[a] Excludes individuals not employed and not looking for work.

results suggest that not pursuing additional schooling after secondary school may make it more difficult to find employment for women but not for men.

Another relevant outcome is the relationship between post-secondary schooling and job type. The analyses described in Chapter Three indicated that about 95 percent of currently employed members in the 1998 cohort were working in the government or in government enterprises. Table 4.2 reports the distribution across different types of employers by whether the individual had any post-secondary schooling. The results indicate that virtually all working members of the 1998 cohort were in a government ministry or a corporation owned by the government. Moreover, working for a given type of employer was not found to be strongly related to having a post-secondary degree.

Table 4.2
Current Type of Employer, 1998 Cohort, by Level of Education

Type of Employer	Percent with Education Level	
	Secondary	More Than Secondary
Government	58	62
Government-owned company	39	33
Private sector	0	2
Other	4	3
Sample size[a]	23	43

[a] Includes only those in overall sample who were currently employed.

For instance, of those working in one of the ministries, 58 percent had only a secondary degree and 62 percent had post-secondary schooling (p = .73).

Although type of employing organization was on average not found to be strongly related to level of schooling, there were important differences in the types of jobs held by Qatari workers who did and did not pursue post-secondary studies. Table 4.3 shows the distribution across occupations by level of education. The results reveal, not surprisingly, that workers with post-secondary schooling were holding jobs that typically require an employee to be well educated. Only 15 percent of workers with no post-secondary education were working as a teacher or in a job that can be classified as professional, compared with 57 percent of individuals with a post-secondary degree (p < .01).[1] In contrast, 28 percent of workers with no post-secondary schooling indicated

Table 4.3
Occupations, 1998 Cohort, by Level of Education

	Percent with Education Level		
Occupation	Secondary	More Than Secondary	Overall
Associate professional	12	13	13
Clerk	28	6	13
Elementary worker	8	0	2
Legislator/senior officer/manager	0	7	5
Military/police	12	9	10
Operator	12	2	5
Professional	15	22	20
Service worker	4	0	1
Teacher	0	35	24
Technician	8	8	8
Sample size[a]	22	42	64

[a] Includes only those in overall sample who provided a job title for their most recent job.

---

[1]   As discussed earlier (and described in more detail in Appendix A), self-reported job titles are classified on the basis of the ISCO-88 guidelines.

that they were working as clerks, compared with 6 percent of workers with post-secondary schooling (p < .05).[2]

Table 4.4 shows the distribution of Qataris across industries by gender and level of education that appears in the 2004 census tabulations. One interesting pattern here is that the percentage of individuals working in public administration falls sharply with level of education: 55 percent of all employees who have only a secondary degree work in public administration compared with 40 percent of employees with post-secondary education. On the other hand, the percentage of individuals working in education jumps from 6 percent of those with a secondary degree to 37 percent of those with a post-secondary degree. Virtually all Qataris working in either of these two sectors are employed by a government ministry. For instance, almost all teachers are employed by the Ministry of Education, and public administration consists of government jobs in other ministries.[3] Thus, although Table 4.2 indicates that the probability of working in a government ministry is not strongly related to educational attainment, the results in Table 4.4 suggest that the *type* of ministry job held is related to educational attainment, with individuals who do not pursue post-secondary studies more likely than those with a post-secondary education to work in public administration.[4]

---

[2]   According to the International Labour Organization's definition, "clerks" are those who store, compute, and retrieve information and perform a number of clerical duties, especially in connection with money-handling operations, travel arrangements, requests for information, and appointments (as of May 23, 2007: http://www.ilo.org/public/english/bureau/stat/isco/isco88/index.htm).

[3]   Individuals employed at the Ministry of Interior as police officers or in the military are classified as working in public administration.

[4]   Note that this pattern is especially strong for women. The percentage of men working in public administration who pursue post-secondary studies and the percentage who do not are similar (55 percent and 59 percent, respectively).

Table 4.4
Industries of Economically Active Qataris Age 15 and Over, by Gender and Level of Education

Industry	Men			Women			Overall		
	Less Than Secondary	Secondary	More Than Secondary	Less Than Secondary	Secondary	More Than Secondary	Less Than Secondary	Secondary	More Than Secondary
Mining and quarrying	7	16	10	2	8	1	6	14	6
Health and social work	2	2	3	14	18	7	3	6	5
Public administration	76	59	55	45	41	24	73	55	40
Education	1	3	11	30	18	64	4	6	37
Other community, social, and personal services	1	3	3	3	4	1	2	3	2
Electricity, gas, and water supply	4	4	3	1	3	0	4	4	2
Other	8	12	14	5	8	3	8	11	9

Percent with Education Level

SOURCE: Planning Council, 2004.

Backgrounds and Attitudes Toward Work and School of Those with Secondary and Post-Secondary Degrees

Information from our 1998 cohort survey sheds light on whether the backgrounds and attitudes of individuals who did not pursue post-secondary schooling differ from those of Qataris who completed additional schooling. In Qatar, a student's major field of study is an important dimension of his or her educational background. Table 4.5 shows that the most popular major among all students was literature, mathematics, and science.[5] However, students who continued their education were considerably less likely than students who did not continue their education to have specialized in this field (41 percent and 64 percent, respectively; p < .05). Even more striking is the fact that only 12 percent of students who did not pursue post-secondary studies had majored in science, compared with 39 percent who did (p < .01). These patterns are not necessarily surprising, however, given that the science major is considered to be the most academically demanding field in Qatari secondary schools. The findings in Table 4.5 strongly suggest that the students who pursue post-secondary studies are the ones who received the most rigorous preparation in secondary school.

Table 4.5
Field of Study, 1998 Cohort, by Level of Education

Field of Study[a]	Percent with Education Level		
	Secondary	More Than Secondary	Overall
Science	12	39	31
Literature, math and science	64	41	48
French literature	17	19	19
Industrial	5	1	2
Commercial	2	0	1
Sample size	34	63	97

[a] As defined by the Ministry of Education.

---

[5] The major fields of study listed in Table 4.5 for secondary school are the categories used by the Ministry of Education. The literature, mathematics, and science field of study has a general liberal arts curriculum, whereas the science field of study includes more-advanced courses in science and mathematics.

We also examined the 1998 cohort's attitudes toward education and work by level of education, but found no significant differences between the two groups. Similarly, the two groups did not differ significantly in terms of the importance they placed on different job characteristics in choosing a job or career.

Reasons for Not Pursuing Post-Secondary Schooling

To better understand the needs of students who do not continue their schooling after secondary school, it is crucial to know their reasons for not continuing. Table 4.6 shows the results from asking the 1998 graduates to indicate which of the reasons listed applied to their decision. Note that because of the small sample size (N = 25), these findings must be interpreted with some caution.[6] The results suggest that poor performance in secondary school represents a serious barrier to pursuing additional schooling. Although only 23 percent (6 respondents) cited "not interested in/did not do well in school" as an important reason, the most commonly cited reason was ineligibility for a scholarship

Table 4.6
Reasons for Not Pursuing Post-Secondary Schooling, 1998 Cohort

Reason	Percent Citing Reason
Unaware of any offerings	26
Available offerings not useful/interesting	16
Too inconvenient	9
Family responsibilities	58
Health problems	0
Not interested in/did not do well in school	23
Wasn't eligible for scholarship	61
Can't afford to pay for it	33
Sample size[a]	25

[a] Includes only those in overall sample who did not pursue post-secondary schooling.

---

[6]   Because the sample size in this analysis was so small, the discussion here uses the raw numbers of respondents who cited a given reason along with the percentages calculated using the sampling weights.

(61 percent; 15 respondents).[7] Assuming that the indicated reason corresponds with actual behavior, this finding suggests that more respondents would have gone to college had they done better in school and thus been eligible for a scholarship. The second most frequently cited reason was family responsibilities (58 percent; 14 respondents). Although it would be interesting to see which gender cited family responsibilities more frequently as a reason for not pursuing further studies, the sample was too small to make a reliable comparison. Fewer than half of the respondents cited any of the other reasons listed in the survey. However, lack of knowledge about post-secondary opportunities was a factor for some respondents, even though there is now a rich array of post-secondary offerings in Qatar.

Twenty-six percent (6 respondents) indicated that they were unaware of any offerings, and another 16 percent (4 respondents) indicated that they found the available offerings not useful/interesting. These results suggest that Qatar may be able to increase the number of students attending post-secondary school simply by providing students with better information on the opportunities available to them.

A sizable fraction of respondents (33 percent; 9 respondents) indicated that they could not afford to pay for additional schooling, suggesting that financial barriers may also be important. This is a surprising finding given that Qatar is a very wealthy country and that Qataris who qualify for QU pay no tuition. Thus, costs are likely pivotal only for those students who are deciding between studying abroad and not pursuing a post-secondary education. This result may explain why just over half of the respondents listed ineligibility for a scholarship as an important reason for not continuing. It is also interesting to note the reasons that were not frequently cited. Only 9 percent cited that pursuing a post-secondary education was too inconvenient, and no one indicated that the reason for non-pursuit was health problems.

Further insight into what influences the decision to pursue or not pursue post-secondary schooling came from examining what the respondents in the survey of 2006 secondary school seniors cited as

---

[7]   This percentage may increase given that Qatar University recently raised its entrance requirements.

being important factors in choosing what they would do after graduating. Table 4.7 shows that students planning and not planning to
pursue further studies generally viewed the same factors as important
in making their decision. One notable difference is in the percentages
citing enjoyment of learning and school as an important factor in their
decision: 82 percent of those intending to go on to post-secondary
studies cited this factor, compared with only 56 percent of those not
intending to go on (p < .01). Another result, consistent with the evidence from the survey of 1998 graduates, is that getting a scholarship
is an important determinant of post-secondary plans for 72 percent of
the sampled students. Even 62 percent of students who do not plan to
pursue further studies cited the importance of receiving a scholarship,
suggesting that some students anticipate being ineligible for a scholarship and therefore do not plan on further education.

Table 4.7
**Factors Influencing Students' Plans to Pursue or Not Pursue Post-Secondary
Schooling, 2006 Cohort**

| Factor | Percent Responding That Factor Is Very or Extremely Important | | |
	Planning Not to Pursue Post-Secondary	Planning to Pursue Post-Secondary	Unsure
Personal interests	87	86	88
Parental advice	95	96	97
Advice from other family members	64	61	50
Advice from friends	44	42	49
Religious beliefs	96	96	96
Societal expectations	74	80	73
Enjoyment of learning and school	56	82	64
Job openings	91	89	88
Whether I get a scholarship	62	81	72
Sample size[a]	71	147	36

[a] Varies slightly from statement to statement.

Possible Benefits from Acquiring Certain Skills

As discussed earlier, policymakers in Qatar are interested in understanding the unmet needs of individuals who do not pursue schooling beyond the secondary level. Acquiring key skills may be one such need. Our survey data allowed us to address this issue because respondents were asked to indicate the skills they thought would help them advance in their current job or get a better job.

The findings, presented in Table 4.8, provide guidance on what skills individuals lacking a post-secondary education would like to acquire. A large majority (82 percent) of the respondents indicated that they would like to improve their English (or some other foreign language) skills, and almost half (45 percent) indicated that basic computer skills would be helpful. The only other skills that at least 10 percent of the respondents said they would like to acquire were advanced com-

Table 4.8
Importance of Different Skills, 1998 Cohort, by Level of Education

Skill	Percent in Education Level Responding That Skill Is Needed to Advance in Current Job or Get a Better Job		
	Secondary	More Than Secondary	Overall
Basic math	7	10	9
Reading and writing	8	22	18
Advanced math	0	8	5
Basic computer skills	45	21	28
Advanced computer skills	18	17	17
Specific technology/equipment	0	8	5
To work in a team	8	15	13
Communicate with outside customers	8	17	14
English/other foreign language	82	36	50
To solve problems	4	18	14
Follow directions from a supervisor	0	13	9
To give directions to other people	0	8	5
Sample size[a]	24	44	68

[a] Includes only those in overall sample who were currently employed.

puter skills (18 percent). Fewer of those expressing a need to acquire these skills were respondents who had post-secondary schooling. For instance, of those with post-secondary schooling, only 36 percent cited a need to improve their foreign language skills, and only 21 percent cited basic computer skills. However, the individuals in this group felt more in need of improving their skills in nearly all the other areas, including communications, problem solving, and both following and giving directions.

Characteristics of Students Planning Not to Pursue Post-Secondary Studies

We also assessed the relationship between educational plans and several background characteristics. As Table 4.9 shows, the characteristic leading to the largest difference is gender: male students in the 2006 cohort constituted 74 percent of the students planning not to pursue a

Table 4.9
Background Characteristics, 2006 Cohort, by Post-Secondary Plan

Characteristic	Percent			
	Planning Not to Pursue Post-Secondary	Planning to Pursue Post-Secondary	Unsure	Overall
Male	74	36	36	48
Field of study				
Literature/humanities	50	44	50	47
Science and math	50	56	50	53
Repeat grade	24	27	12	24
At least father has post-secondary education	15	25	36	23
At least mother has post-secondary education	12	17	20	16
Aware of scholarship opportunities	97	95	90	95
Sample size[a]	71	147	37	255

[a] Varies slightly for each characteristic because of missing data.

post-secondary education, and they constituted only 36 percent of the students who were planning to go on (p < .01). In addition, students planning to continue their education were somewhat more likely than those not planning to continue their education to have a father with a post-secondary degree (25 percent versus 15 percent; p = .10). However, the differences for the other characteristics were small and not statistically significant.

Table 4.10 examines whether post-secondary plans are associated with the type of organization in which the respondent would like to work.[8] The results show that students not planning to pursue post-secondary studies were more likely to prefer working in government ministries and less likely to want to work in a government-owned company than were students with plans to continue their studies. And even though very few respondents indicated an interest in working in a privately owned company, it is noteworthy that not one of them was planning to pursue post-secondary studies. In other words, whatever interest there is in private-sector employment appears to be limited to individuals who plan to pursue a post-secondary education. These survey results in and of themselves are insufficient to shed light on whether this finding stems from lack of interest or lack of opportunities, but we see it

Table 4.10
Desired Type of Employer, 2006 Cohort, by Post-Secondary Plan

Type of Employer Desired	Percent			
	Planning Not to Pursue Post-Secondary	Planning to Pursue Post-Secondary	Unsure	Overall
Ministry	65	50	42	54
Govt.-owned company	16	28	21	24
Private religious organization/charity	11	7	17	10
Private company	0	6	0	3
Unsure	7	8	19	10
Sample size	63	131	35	229

[8]   Only seven (four females and three males) of 260 respondents reported that they did not plan to get a job.

as likely stemming from both. The evidence from our employer interviews (discussed in Chapter Three) suggests that private-sector employers do not hire individuals lacking post-secondary schooling for the
types of highly respected jobs that young Qataris expect to be given.
Regardless of the cause, however, the finding suggests that policymakers will have difficulty increasing the number of Qataris working in the
private sector who lack a post-secondary degree. This will prove especially challenging with regard to drawing Qatari men into the private
sector, since men are so much less likely than women to pursue a post-
secondary education.[9]

The occupation someone would most like to have is also related
to educational plans. As Table 4.11 shows, about two-thirds of the secondary school seniors were unsure about the type of job they wanted to
have. However, those students who planned to pursue a post-secondary
education and also indicated a job they would like to have tended to

Table 4.11
Desired Occupation, 2006 Cohort, by Post-Secondary Plan

Occupation	Percent			
	Planning Not to Pursue Post-Secondary	Planning to Pursue Post-Secondary	Unsure	Overall
Associate professional	2	2	4	2
Clerk	0	1	0	1
Engineer	0	5	0	3
Legislator/senior officer/manager	2	7	6	5
Military/police	24	6	2	11
Professional	2	11	7	8
Service worker	0	0	3	1
Teacher	0	6	3	4
Unsure	70	62	73	66
Sample size	63	126	35	224

---

[9]   Of the nine students in this survey who indicated that they wanted to work in the private
sector, eight were female. In our 1998 cohort survey, however, all those who worked in the
private sector were male.

list occupations such as engineering, teaching, and senior manager, all of which probably require at least a university degree. In sharp contrast, almost all students not planning to go on to post-secondary schooling and who also indicated a desired job listed an occupation related to either the military or the police, which suggests that these occupations are perceived as attractive opportunities by students (particularly males) who do not plan to continue beyond secondary schooling.

Summary and Key Findings

This chapter has examined the needs and experiences of secondary school seniors who are not planning to pursue post-secondary studies and of secondary school graduates who did not pursue post-secondary studies. These individuals make up a sizable portion of the young Qatari population, especially the male population. Our survey evidence suggests that Qataris who do not seek a post-secondary education have markedly different experiences in the labor market than do Qataris who continue their studies beyond secondary school. Additionally, our results shed light on factors that influence an individual's decision not to pursue a post-secondary education, and suggest unmet needs that these individuals may have.

Our key findings from this examination are as follows:

1. Women with post-secondary schooling are more likely to be employed than are women without this schooling, but no such relationship exists for men.
2. Individuals without a post-secondary degree are less likely to work as professionals and more likely to work as clerks or in the military or police than are individuals who have a post-secondary education.
3. The most frequently given reasons for not pursuing a post-secondary education were ineligibility for a scholarship and family responsibilities.
4. Workers without a post-secondary education indicated that training in English and, to a lesser extent, basic computer skills

would be helpful for either advancing in their current job or getting a better job in the future.

5. Secondary school seniors who were not planning to pursue post-secondary studies were more likely to want to work in a government ministry and less likely to want to work in a government-owned or privately owned company than were students who intended to pursue post-secondary studies.

6. Almost all secondary school seniors who were not planning to seek a post-secondary education and who stated a desired occupation wanted to be in the police or military. This suggests that these types of jobs are seen as an attractive alternative to pursuing post-secondary studies, especially for males.

7. An examination of attitudes toward work and preferences in job characteristics did not reveal any strong differences between Qataris who plan to pursue or do pursue post-secondary schooling and those who do not.

CHAPTER FIVE

Education and Training Provision

Previous chapters explored the occupations and skills considered vital to the growth and development of Qatar's economy and society, as well as the education and training needed to secure employment in these occupations. This section examines the extent to which the requisite education and training are available to Qataris, and whether further investment in education and training is required.

We begin by describing the current post-secondary education environment, including the institutions operating in Qatar and the accompanying degrees and fields of study. We then discuss the program for study abroad and the scholarship system, two important elements of students' access to higher education. The largest training providers operating in Qatar and the types of programs they offer are discussed next, after which we explore how the current education and training offerings relate to the demand for skills and occupations (this analysis includes a look at whether opportunities for education and training differ by gender). Finally, we compare data from our inventory of post-secondary education and training offerings with the education and training requirements identified in Chapter Three in order to identify gaps in the post-secondary education and training offerings. We also discuss the issue of required investments.

What Higher Education Programs Are Being Offered?

Background on Higher Education Investment

The Qatari government began investing in higher education more than 30 years ago, in 1973, when it opened the publicly funded College of Education that would expand and become Qatar University (see discussion in Chapter Two). Qatar University provides free tuition for Qatari students and students from the other GCC countries who meet the entrance requirements and maintain a 2.0 grade point average. The University also offers scholarships to students from Arab and Islamic countries (Foreign Information Agency, undated).

The government has invested in higher education in other ways, as well. Since the 1970s, Qatar has had a scholarship system designed to send students abroad for undergraduate and graduate programs not available locally. In addition, post-secondary training is provided by government ministries, government-owned companies, and several non-profit and for-profit providers.

Over the past decade, investment in education and training has intensified. In 1995, the Qatar Foundation was founded by Emiri decree with the mission to provide educational opportunities and improve the quality of life for the people of Qatar and the region (Qatar Foundation, 2007b). The Qatar Foundation's flagship project is Education City, which was officially inaugurated in 2003. The Foundation invited world-class universities to operate campuses in Qatar (Foreign Information Agency, undated).[1] In 1998, Virginia Commonwealth University School of the Arts opened its design school. Weill Cornell Medical College began offering its medical programs in 2002. Texas A&M University followed in 2003, offering undergraduate degree programs in petroleum, chemical, electrical, and mechanical engineering. Carnegie Mellon University started teaching classes in 2004, bringing to Doha its programs in computer science and business. Georgetown University started its foreign service programs in August 2005

---

[1]   The branch campus model establishes complete interchangeability between an institution's main campus and its branch campus in terms of educational offerings, requirements, degrees, etc. VCU, the first Education City institution, was not originally set up as a branch campus, but it later conformed to the branch campus model.

(Foreign Information Agency, undated). Future plans for Education City include the establishment of programs in journalism and communications, as well as an Islamic studies center (Qatar Foundation, 2007a). A variety of government-sponsored scholarships (discussed in detail later in this chapter) are available to Qatari students to cover the tuition and other costs of attending Education City campuses.

Outside of Education City, CHN University Netherlands, which has operated in Doha since 2000, offers bachelor's degrees in hospitality management and tourism management. Many students at CHN University Netherlands are sponsored by companies, ministries, and other organizations. The College of the North Atlantic–Qatar, a Canadian institution, opened in 2002 and offers various two- and three-year diploma and certificate programs in engineering, business, health sciences, IT, and related fields designed for industrial, commercial, and government organizations. A majority of students attending this institution are sponsored by employers.

Enrollment

Table 5.1 shows student enrollment in four-year post-secondary institutions in Qatar.[2] Qatar University enrolls the vast majority (91 percent) of students attending four-year institutions. Seventy-one percent of all students enrolled in four-year institutions are Qataris, and less than one-quarter (23 percent) of Qatari students are male. Qatar University has the biggest Qatari/non-Qatari student ratio (74 percent), and Weill Cornell Medical College has the smallest (20 percent). CHN University Netherlands has the largest male-female ratio of Qatari students (56 percent), whereas no Qatari males are enrolled in design majors at Virginia Commonwealth University.

Fields of Study and Degrees Offered in Qatar

Table 5.2 shows the fields of study and degrees available from post-secondary institutions in Qatar. A wide array of study areas is offered, and this array provides students with a wide range of skills to take to the labor market. (Appendix B lists the detailed post-secondary fields

---

[2]   CNA, a two-year institution, enrolls 1,550 students.

Table 5.1
Student Enrollment in Four-Year Post-Secondary Institutions in Qatar, 2005–2006

Institution	All Students		Qatari Students	
	Number Enrolled	% of Total Enrollment	Number Enrolled	% of Total Enrollment
Qatar University	7,660	91	5,671	74
CHN Univ. Netherlands	257	3	96	37
Virginia Commonwealth	181	2	121	67
Weill Cornell Medical College	135	2	27	20
Texas A&M University	140	2	88	63
Carnegie Mellon University	47	1	18	38
Georgetown University	25	0	12	48
Total	8,445	100	6,033	71

NOTE: Percentages shown have been rounded.

Table 5.2
Degrees and Fields of Study Offered in Qatar

Degree	Institution	Fields of Study
2-year diploma/ certificate	College of the North Atlantic	Engineering, business, health sciences, IT, trades
Bachelor's	Texas A&M University (EC)	Engineering
	Virginia Commonwealth University (EC)	Design
	Carnegie Mellon University (EC)	Business, computer science
	Georgetown University (EC)	Foreign service
	Qatar University	Education, arts and sciences, engineering, business, law, Sharia and Islamic studies
	CHN University Netherlands	Hospitality and tourism
Graduate	Weill Cornell Medical College (EC)	Doctor of Medicine
	Texas A&M University (EC)	Master's degrees in engineering beginning in 2007
	Qatar University	Post-graduate diplomas in education; master's in business administration

NOTE: "(EC)" indicates that the institution is in Education City.

of study and degree offerings in Qatar.) Important points worth noting about this substantial variety of fields and degrees are as follows:

- The study fields available at Qatar University constitute a broad spectrum of areas. And because Qatar University's admission requirements are considerably lower than those of the Education City campuses, Qatar University is available to many secondary school graduates with university aspirations.
- The study fields available at CHN University Netherlands are narrow and aimed at training students for specific fields in a single industry (e.g., hospitality management).
- The only graduate degree currently offered in Education City is the doctor of medicine (M.D.) degree at Weill Cornell Medical College. In the 2007–2008 academic year, Texas A&M will begin offering master's degrees in engineering and science.
- Qatar University is primarily an undergraduate institution and only offers graduate study in education and business.
- Because Qatar University and the Education City campuses currently offer only a few graduate programs, most students who want to earn a graduate degree must go abroad. This constitutes a roadblock for some individuals, particularly women, who are unable to study abroad because of family and cultural considerations.

Admission to the Education City campuses is very competitive; only a small minority of students in Qatar (or anywhere else) are academically qualified for admittance. The fields of study available in Education City cover areas of primary interest to employers. While the quality is high and the available degrees are relevant to the labor market, some fields that may be of interest to high-achieving students are not offered (e.g., liberal arts and sciences).

In addition to offering certificates or degrees in various fields of study, these institutions cater to students needing remedial work to make the most of their higher-education experience. The College of the North Atlantic offers Access programs, which are developmental programs that students may enter prior to full admission in regular certificate/diploma-level programs. Qatar University's Foundation Program provides remedial course work for newly arrived students to help them meet the University's minimum course requirements. Students in the Foundation Program must successfully complete course work in the English language, mathematics, and computers. Students able to pass the English language, mathematics, and computer placement tests may receive full or partial exemption from the Foundation Program. The Foundation Program also prepares students to meet specific entrance requirements established by the individual Qatar University colleges.

At the other end of the spectrum, the Qatar Foundation supports the Academic Bridge Program, which is designed to prepare exceptional secondary school graduates in Qatar and elsewhere in the region for study at highly selective English-language universities in Education City and abroad. Students study English, mathematics, computers, and skills for university success. Male and female students in the Academic Bridge Program attend classes together, and all courses are taught in English. The program began in 2001 and is based in Education City; it currently enrolls 220 students, mostly from Qatar.

The remedial programs currently offered serve particular students who have already met basic university entry requirements but need additional preparation. These programs do not help low-performing secondary students who do not qualify for Qatar University, or adults who want to pursue university studies later in life. Qatar University does offer a continuing education program, but with the exception of its English language courses, it is designed for narrow, job-specific training. In addition, recent reforms at Qatar University reaffirm its primary mission as an undergraduate academic institution. A traditional community college may be the best way to address the post-secondary education and training needs of some segments of Qatari society. Such a college would provide remedial programs for weaker students—those needing to strengthen their academic preparation before beginning undergraduate studies—and an entry point to university for adults wishing to pursue a degree or to improve or acquire skills. (We explore this possibility more fully later.)

Scholarship System and Study Abroad

Qatar provides many scholarship opportunities for highly qualified students who want to pursue post-secondary education in Qatar or abroad. These scholarships are an important vehicle for developing skills in Qatar because they can be targeted to meet particular economic or social needs. Thus, they are an essential part of the post-secondary education landscape.

Higher Education Institute Scholarships. The HEI was established under the SEC in March 2005 to help students make educational and career choices based on their interests, abilities, and values, as well as the needs of the Qatari labor market. One of the HEI's primary roles is managing the scholarship system. It administers scholarships; identifies top universities, degree programs, and short-term professional development courses in Qatar and around the world for HEI scholarship applicants; and determines the targeted specialties for scholarship recipients (high-demand occupations, such as medicine, engineering, finance, and economics, currently have high priority).

The HEI administers a previous (pre-HEI) scholarship program (now closed to newcomers) and the following five new scholarship programs, three of which (the Emiri, the National, and the Employee scholarship programs) include both undergraduate and graduate study options:[3]

- *Emiri Scholarship:* Awarded to exceptional students—those with significant academic achievements and the potential to become national leaders—who have been accepted into one of 50 top institutions worldwide as determined by the HEI. There is no predetermined number of scholarships available; they are awarded to everyone who qualifies. Out of 114 recipients for the 2005–2006 academic year, six (four males, two females) are studying abroad; the rest are studying at Education City institutions.
- *National Scholarship:* Intended for students who have the potential to become future business and professional leaders in targeted

---

[3] For further information on scholarships, see Scholarship Guide 2006–2007 (Higher Education Institute, 2006).

fields in Qatar and have been accepted into one of 250 HEI-approved institutions. As with the Emiri Scholarship, everyone who qualifies receives a scholarship. In the 2005–2006 academic year, 204 students received this scholarship.

- *Employee Scholarship:* Offered in partnership with public and private employers in Qatar to enable high-potential employees to pursue additional education and advanced training at HEI-approved universities in areas of critical importance to Qatar.
- *Diploma Scholarship:* Available to students seeking technical and specialized diplomas that are in demand in Qatar's labor market, such as nursing and aviation. These scholarships are currently available for the College of the North Atlantic.
- *Pre-College Grant* (for English- and non-English-speaking countries): Supports students who need additional academic preparation prior to beginning their post-secondary studies. It is available for programs such as the Academic Bridge Program and is offered to students with the expectation that they will be accepted into an HEI-approved college or university.

Applicants to the scholarship programs must be Qatari citizens, have a pre-determined minimum score on a relevant English language test (for some universities), meet certain criteria regarding past academic performance, and agree to work in an area of importance to Qatar upon graduation for a time equal to the length of the scholarship (except in the case of the Pre-College Grant).

Several other scholarship programs are under consideration and may be implemented in the near future: Loan-Based Scholarships for non-Qataris accepted at institutions deemed prestigious by the HEI, as well as in approved programs in Education City and Qatar University; Professional Development Grants to assist individuals admitted to short-term study programs with the goal of improving job skills or developing new job skills for career advancement or job transition. Other financial assistance may be available as well to help Qataris participate in internationally recognized academic or professional development opportunities, such as the Fulbright program or special internships (Supreme Education Council, 2005).

Table 5.3 shows numbers of students enrolled in HEI scholarship programs for the 2005–2006 school year. There are 1,445 students enrolled in all scholarship programs, including 604 students with the pre-HEI scholarships.

Table 5.4 provides a breakdown of students by field of study for the fields with the highest concentration of HEI scholarship recipients. The highest concentrations of students are in different areas of engineering (119 students); medicine (134, including dentistry); business, finance, and economics (98); law (72); graphic design and fine arts and interior design (56); and education (42).

The HEI scholarship programs cover scholar stipend, tuition and fees, and health insurance, as well as allowances for spouse, children, books, computer, and other expenses. About 57 percent of scholarship expenses are directed for tuition and fees. Those studying abroad also receive travel expenses and allowances for clothing and relocation.

The HEI is not the only agency sponsoring scholarships. The Qatar Foundation provides scholarships for "Children of Qatari Women." All students who are accepted into an Education City institution, have Qatari mothers, and submit an application receive one of these scholarships. The Qatar Foundation also administers the Hamad Bin

Table 5.3
Numbers of Students in Higher Education Institute Scholarship Programs

Scholarship Program	Continuing Students	New Students	Total
Emiri	59	55	114
National	150	54	204
Employee	110	9	119
Pre-college (Academic Bridge Program)	0	127	127
Diploma: CNA	66	24	90
Diploma: Qatar Aeronautical College	92	95	187
Pre-HEI: USA/Canada/Australia	87	0	87
Pre-HEI: Europe	256	0	256
Pre-HEI: Middle East/Asia	261	0	261
Total	1,081	364	1,445

SOURCE: Supreme Education Council, 2005.

Table 5.4
Highest Concentrations in Higher Education Institute Scholarships, by Field of Study

Field of Study	Bachelor's	Master's	Doctoral	Specialist Training	Total
Medicine	82	2	6	23	113
Law	45	22	5		72
Graphic design, fine arts and interior design	56				56
Communication/electronic engineering	36	12			48
Education	6	19	17		42
Business administration	31	9	3		43
Computer science	29	1			30
Finance/financial management	16	8	2		26
Computer engineering	22				22
Dentistry	20	1			21
Political science	14	4	1		19
Industrial engineering	18				18
Electrical engineering	18				18
Petroleum engineering	13				13
Investment management/banking	6	2	2		10
International relations	9	1			10
Economics	8	1	1		10
Marketing	9				9
Total	438	82	37	23	580

SOURCE: Supreme Education Council, 2005.

Khalifa Financial Aid Program for students enrolled at an Education City institution. Funded by the Emir, this program addresses the needs of students who qualify but do not have the financial means, and/or children of expatriates who have been living in Qatar for a long time or have provided special services to the country. The funding is provided in exchange for either a period of post-graduate paid employment at an organization in Qatar (as designated by the Qatar Foundation) or reimbursement to the Foundation of the full amount of financial aid received. This program covers tuition and may also cover boarding fees, health expenses, reasonable expenses for travel to home country only, reasonable personal expenses, and other expenses (Qatar Foundation, 2007c).

In addition, the Student Employment program helps students in Education City gain work experience and enables them to earn money while doing so. All students in Education City may work in any of the branch campuses or centers within Education City. To qualify for this program, a student must be enrolled in one of the branch campuses, the Academic Bridge Program, or Qatar Academy (a private school in Doha). Students in this program may work up to 20 hours per week while classes are in session, and 40 hours per week during class breaks (Qatar Foundation, 2007d).

Value of Study Abroad Program. As part of our data collection for this project, we interviewed key employers and other stakeholders to learn their perceptions of the advantages and disadvantages associated with study abroad and with post-secondary study in Qatar. Employers saw a role both for strengthening and expanding post-secondary options in Qatar and for continuing to send students abroad for higher education. Both options convey distinct benefits to students and to society.

The most cited benefit for sending students out of the country was the broadening effect it has on them both intellectually and culturally. They are exposed to new ideas and ways of doing things. The standards of foreign institutions are high, and students learn to be more independent. Interviewees saw Qatar as a developing country in many ways, and viewed the attitudes and professional skills of Qataris as needing to rise to international standards. Studying abroad was seen as a way to help students develop the needed attitudes and skills.

Employers and education leaders also said that even though studying abroad is more expensive than studying at Qatar University, the long-term value to students and to Qatari society from the experiences and perspectives that students gain is beyond the accounting costs. A common theme among employers and other stakeholders was that the important issue in deciding the value of sending students abroad is not cost-effectiveness or quantity of graduates but, rather, *quality* of graduates.

Employers and other stakeholders also thought there was an important role for Education City in the training of Qatari students. Education City clearly provides more opportunities for high-quality post-secondary education for the most-able students, but there are societal benefits besides. Education City represents a change in attitude about the importance of education in Qatar. Together with the heightened awareness of education promoted by the ongoing K–12 education reform, the availability of more high-quality educational options makes students more aware of the importance of education, what options are available, and what preparation is necessary to take advantage of those options.

Some individuals we interviewed were concerned that inordinate amounts of resources are being devoted to educating the elite students, and that more can be done to strengthen the options for the remaining, majority of students, such as those at Qatar University. Moreover, some interviewees discussed the unique role of Qatar University in maintaining Qatari culture and values. For example, the Education City university branches provide education in a mixed-gender environment, and interviewees believed it is important to maintain some university options that permit study in a single-gender environment. Some women do not want to study in a mixed-gender environment and are therefore unlikely to pursue post-secondary education unless a single-gender option is available.

In sum, the employers and other stakeholders expressed a wide range of opinions about higher education in Qatar and abroad. Each of these has advantages, and each has a role in educating different types of students and providing different types of cultural experiences. In the cases of study abroad and Education City, there are societal benefits of education that are an important element of helping Qatar adapt to an increasingly global society while maintaining its important cultural values and characteristics.

Provision of Post-Secondary Training

The numerous training providers in Qatar are from all sectors, including the government, government-owned companies, and non-government organizations (both for-profit and not-for-profit). This section discusses some of the largest training providers, including some used by the SEC. (Appendix C provides additional information on selected training providers.)

Government Training Providers. Among government agencies, the Ministry of Civil Service Affairs and Housing (MoCSAH) is the largest sponsor of training. Two training organizations are associated with MoCSAH, the Institute of Administrative Development (IAD) and the Training Center; MoCSAH provides funding for the first and operates the second. These two training organizations serve different groups: The IAD provides training for government employees, and the Training Center prepares secondary school graduates for entry-level jobs in the private sector.

The IAD started with 22 programs in 1997 and currently has 160 tailor-made programs in management, finance, information technology (IT), English language, banking, insurance, tourism, etc. From 1997 to 2005, the IAD trained 11,000 government employees, of which 4,500 were female. The most popular training programs are management programs, followed by finance and IT. The human resource department of any government institution selects trainees and sends a training request to IAD. Before taking up positions, new job holders may spend up to six months at IAD. Individuals already working in the government can also apply for training programs, if their ministry agrees. However, the final approval has to come from MoCSAH.

The IAD has 22 faculty members. It hires as trainers people from the United Kingdom, the United States, and other Anglophone countries, and people with degrees from universities in which courses are taught in English. The program is recognized regionally by Egypt's Arab Administrative Development Organization and internationally by Canada's Public Administration Institute. The IAD awards certificates at the end of each training program. Taking IAD training courses can be an important factor for promotion, and most employees return to the IAD for additional training courses.

The mission of the Training Center is to prepare Qatari secondary school graduates for entry-level jobs in the private sector and to help the government meet Qatarization goals. A small fraction of students are college graduates. Established in 2000, the Training Center targets Qataris who have not been employed and would normally be unable to work in the private sector because of poor performance at school or because their area of study is not in demand. The Center helps such individuals gain vocational qualifications and other skills needed to join the private sector. A number of primary-school teachers have enrolled as well, to improve their abilities in classroom management.

The length of instruction is 1.5 to 2 years split into two phases. The first phase is a foundational year in which students undergo extensive courses in English language, computing, and basic skills. The second phase prepares trainees to get a Business and Technology Education Council Intermediate Certificate in Principles of Work Level 1 or Level 2, which are internationally recognized awards.

The Center collects information about job vacancies and works in conjunction with sponsors from the private as well as the public sector. These organizations have incentives to provide training to those individuals who are not qualified in order to meet Qatarization goals. Sponsors provide trainees with financial incentives/stipends, mentoring services on specific jobs, and a suitable workplace so that they can gain work experience; trainees cannot graduate without having work experience. The Center provides sponsors with progress reports on a regular basis. After the program is finished, the employer decides whether or not to hire the trainee.

As of November 2005, the Center had trained 616 Qatari females and 435 Qatari males. Current enrollments are heavily skewed toward female Qataris: At the time of this study, roughly 90 percent of the class was female. The Center is encouraging more males to attend its program so that it can help increase their self-confidence by involving them in its Special Services Preparation program, which includes training in disaster management, first aid, personal safety, and social responsibilities.

A side note to these government-sponsored training programs is their "hidden cost"—the government paid for the secondary schooling of many individuals who are also receiving training from IAD and the Training Center. In effect, the government is paying twice to train the trainees.

To gain some perspective on the size of these hidden costs, we estimated the number of individuals the IAD and the Training Center have trained and the approximate cost per person. Through 2005, the number of people trained by the IAD and Training Center together was about 12,000. As an estimate of the cost per person we used the cost of an English language course offered by ELS Language Centers, which provides English language training around the world, including in Doha.[4] For an "intensive" English language course (30 lessons per week for four weeks), the cost is about $1,400 U.S. dollars (USD), or 5,096.42 Qatari riyals (QAR). Therefore, the approximate hidden cost of training through 2005, based on these assumptions, was $16,800,000 USD (12,000 x $1,400), or QAR 61,157,040. Using a more conservative cost estimate of $1,000 per course, which is the approximate price for a semi-intensive course (20 lessons per week for four weeks), the approximate hidden cost of training goes to $12,000,000 USD, or QAR 43,683,600. While these calculations are very approximate, they nonetheless demonstrate that the hidden costs associated with training individuals a second time represents a large government expense.

Training Provided by Government-Owned Companies. Among government-owned companies, Qatar Petroleum is the largest training provider. It provides and/or sponsors a wide range of training programs for its existing and prospective employees. At present, it funds 40 students in the Academic Bridge Program, more than 700 students at the College of the North Atlantic, and 70 students at Qatar University, as well as students in other post-secondary programs in Qatar and abroad. The company has a liaison officer who actively cooperates with the post-secondary institutions—for example, through involvement in curriculum development, membership in boards of trustees, arrangement of summer internships and course projects in coordination with the company, and provision of state-of-the-art technology.

Qatar Petroleum also trains secondary school graduates for technical and clerical jobs, trains employee-level staff to enhance and develop their performance standards as part of their career progres-

---

[4]   ELS Language Centers teach languages under the auspices of Study in the USA, an education guide for international students. Information on the centers is available at http://www.studyusa.com/factshts/els.asp.

sion, arranges English language courses for employees and trainees at all levels, and manages various long-term academic programs.[5]

Private Training Providers. Non-governmental training providers, both for-profit and not-for-profit, train numerous people in Qatar each year. (Appendix C highlights five of these training providers.) One of these companies, New Horizons, trains on average 1,000 individuals per year in IT and business. It offers diplomas in a number of areas, such as administration, public relations and marketing, office management, and basic computer maintenance. Hi Tech, another private company, also trains about 1,000 people each year. It offers the Hi Tech international diploma, which certifies competency in the subjects offered: English language, communication, and general office and financial management. The ELS Language Center and the British Council each train approximately 5,000 people per year in English language skills.

Quality of Training. Although numerous training providers operate in Qatar, there are few direct measures for assessing the quality of the training they offer.[6] We can make the following inferences based on indirect data, however.

First, the non-governmental providers of training are exposed to the competitive forces of the marketplace. If the training they provide is not useful, people will stop seeking their services. Several of the non-governmental training providers have trained 1,000 or more people a year for several years, which suggests that the training they provide is valuable. The government-owned companies that provide training, such as Qatar Petroleum, operate as private companies and thus are also subject to market forces. These companies thus have their own incentive to develop training programs that are demonstrated to make their employees more productive.

---

[5]   Further information on Qatar Petroleum training programs is available at http://www.qatarization.com.qa/qatarization/qat_web.nsf/web/training.

[6]   The Higher Education Institute is currently carrying out an inventory of private training providers in Qatar and aims to develop a system of standards and certification to help regulate their operation.

Second, most of the training providers, including the governmental providers, train their students for certification in internationally recognized programs. To the extent that these international certificates are actually linked to internationally accepted standards, the trainees who receive the certificates are gaining valuable skills.

Do Offerings Relate to Demand for Skills in Specific Occupations/Sectors?

As discussed in Chapter Three, the most important employment in the future for Qatari males will be in professional, technician, and sales and service worker occupations. This is true for Qatari females as well, except that females will be more likely than males to find employment in clerical jobs and in professional jobs in the government. Most of the demand is in mid- or higher-level positions in specific technical areas— such as IT specialists, managers or administrators, customer service representatives, security and finance specialists, and engineers. Individuals with post-secondary education will be especially in demand.

Earlier in this chapter, we discussed the ability of data collected in our inventory of post-secondary education and training offerings to shed light on the extent to which existing institutions and programs are likely to meet current and future education and training demands. Overall, there is good coverage already in many of the high-demand fields considered important to the labor market both now and in the future. At the two-year diploma/certificate level, there are numerous training opportunities for individuals who want to pursue training in high-demand areas. The College of the North Atlantic provides training in the relevant technical fields (chemical, electronics, mechanical engineering, telecommunications technician), as well as in business administration and management, including office administration, which was mentioned as particularly important for women. It also offers certificates in IT training. Further, as discussed earlier, the IAD and the Training Center provide training in numerous areas to large numbers of people. And Qatar Petroleum provides and/or sponsors training in a wide range of areas to hundreds of current and prospective employees.

There currently is ample opportunity to study such high-demand fields as engineering, computer science, and business at both the Education City campuses and Qatar University at the undergraduate level (see Table 5.2, above). Opportunities to pursue graduate studies in the high-demand fields within Qatar are limited, however: an M.D. is offered at Weill Cornell Medical College and a master's of business administration at Qatar University. And beginning in 2007, Texas A&M will offer a master's of engineering and a master's of science degree. Students able to participate in the study abroad program can, of course, pursue their graduate studies at foreign universities; but students who cannot leave Qatar have very limited opportunities to pursue a graduate degree. This deficiency in opportunities for those who cannot go abroad disproportionately affects women, who are less likely than men to study abroad because of family and cultural considerations.

To summarize, the post-secondary education and training options available at the diploma/certificate and undergraduate-degree level are related to skills in occupations that are and will in the future be in high demand in the labor market. There is a post-secondary education gap, however, in the opportunities available for pursuing graduate studies in high-demand fields in Qatar. Given the considerable resources required to operate a high-quality doctoral degree program, the likely limited number of students academically prepared for doctoral study in Qatar, and the relatively low demand in Qatar for doctorates, the focus of new graduate programs will likely be on master's degrees in career-related fields that are in high demand in the labor market (e.g., business, IT, and engineering).

How Do Offerings Relate to Demand for Skills?

Several training facilities in Qatar are designed to teach English and other broad skills. In addition to teaching general English language usage, some facilities, such as the ELS Language Center, teach specialized English skills (e.g., English for business). Some of the main training providers teach communication skills as well as the English language, and at least one, New Horizons, provides training in workplace behavior, which is one of the "soft skills" that employers indicated were very important yet lacking in many job candidates and employees.

One potential offering not readily available in Qatar is general academic skills (except for English) and remedial academic course work to strengthen an individual's academic background and increase the likelihood that he or she will be admitted to a university and, once admitted, will perform well. Such an offering could benefit recent secondary school graduates not academically prepared for college, as well as adults who want to pursue post-secondary studies for the first time or return to finish studies begun earlier to enhance their position in the labor market. As discussed earlier, there are remedial education programs operating in Qatar, but they focus on specific areas or on students who have already met post-secondary enrollment requirements. At present, the opportunities for students who have not met enrollment requirements and cannot do so without remedial academic course work are limited.

Do Offered Opportunities Differ by Gender?

In considering the post-secondary education and training opportunities in Qatar, it is important to account for differences between males and females in terms of the propensity to gain further education and training, success at completing such programs, and types of education and training pursued. Traditionally, males are outnumbered by females in completing secondary school, twice as many males as females fail examinations, and the school dropout rate is three times higher for males than for females (Planning Council, 2005). Further, of those individuals age 19 through 26, only 27 percent of males are enrolled in school, compared with 43 percent of females (Planning Council, 2005). In the 2005–2006 school year, males accounted for less than 17 percent of Qataris enrolled at Qatar University. These statistics, and the findings reported in earlier chapters, indicate that females on average are more engaged and successful in their educational endeavors than males are. It is therefore important to understand whether females have the same educational opportunities as their male counterparts.

Most post-secondary education and training offerings are open to both men and women. The exceptions are a few areas within the sciences at Qatar University that have formal gender restrictions making them open either only to men or only to women, but these are not in high-demand fields. Specifically, bachelor of science degrees in geology, agricultural science, and the double major of geography and urban planning are open only to men at Qatar University, whereas degrees in biomedical science and in food science and nutrition are granted only to women. These differences are likely related to employment opportunities that traditionally have been open solely to men and solely to women in Qatar. Degrees in areas of importance to employers—such as engineering, computer science, and business—are granted to both men and women.

Some job training programs are also open only to men or women. In this case, the gender restrictions stem from cultural restrictions on the types of employment that men and women are to pursue. For example, the firefighter and security training programs offered by Qatar Petroleum are open only to men, and the clerical preparation program is designed for women only.

With respect to post-secondary education, a subtle issue is leading to a gender discrepancy in opportunity. Namely, because of family and cultural considerations, the opportunities for high-achieving students in Qatar to pursue high-quality four-year degrees in fields not currently offered at Education City campuses are more limited for women than for men. For example, if a talented young woman and a talented young man were both interested in studying humanities, which is currently not offered in Education City, their options would be to study at Qatar University or abroad. For young women, however, the likelihood of going abroad to study is less than it is for young men, because of family and cultural considerations. Because this situation may keep young women from pursuing the education needed for high-demand occupations, special attention should be given to making opportunities available to them locally.

Are There Gaps in the Offerings?

Our examination of the post-secondary education and training data suggested three areas in which current offerings do not meet the needs of the labor market. Moreover, our discussion of the available offerings in Qatar suggested that any identification of educational gaps should consider how the needs of specific groups of individuals are being met. We found that post-secondary options are available, to greater and lesser extents, to four specific groups of individuals:

1. *High achievers:* Secondary school graduates who qualify to go abroad, study at Education City or Qatar University, and potentially pursue graduate studies.
2. *University-ready:* Secondary school graduates who qualify for study at Qatar University.
3. *Not ready:* Secondary school graduates who need remediation before pursuing a post-secondary education.
4. *Adults:* Any adult person wishing to pursue learning for career or individual reasons or needing remediation before pursuing university studies.

The first three categories all correspond to secondary school graduates, who were the primary population of interest for this study. In addition, our review indicated that males and females have different needs and aspirations that must be considered. An analysis considering the groups and the gender differences together pointed to the following gaps in post-secondary offerings:

- Limited opportunities for students who need remedial academic course work before they can be admitted to a university. These students include those in the not-ready group; they also include older adults who decide to pursue a post-secondary education.
- Limited choices for high-achieving students in Qatar, especially women, who want to pursue high-quality four-year degrees other than those currently offered in Education City.
- Lack of master's degrees in career-related fields in Qatar. Master's degrees in such fields as engineering, business, and computer sci-

ence would provide skills valuable to the labor market. This gap affects high-achieving students.

The options for addressing these gaps in the provision of education are discussed fully in Chapter Six.

Summary and Key Findings

This chapter has examined the extent to which existing post-secondary institutions in Qatar meet the nation's education and training needs. Overall, we found numerous relevant post-secondary offerings in high-demand fields at the two-year certificate/diploma and undergraduate-degree levels, but very few offerings at the graduate level. We also found numerous entities in Qatar that provide training in most skill areas of importance to the labor market. In spite of overall good coverage in important education and training areas, however, there are gaps in provision that may need to be addressed.

Our key findings from this examination are as follows:

1. At the undergraduate level, the local offerings of Qatar University and the Education City campuses provide opportunities for both university-ready and high-achieving students to pursue degrees in high-demand areas at levels that match these students' preparation and ability.
2. The HEI offers numerous scholarship opportunities for students of different abilities to study abroad. This allows students to study a variety of fields at the best university to which they can gain admission, unconstrained by the fields offered in Qatar. This is particularly important at the graduate level, because few graduate programs are available in Qatar.
3. A review of the largest training providers identified numerous entities that provide training, including government ministries, government-owned companies, and private organizations, both for-profit and not-for-profit. The training provided covers many skills that are highly valued in the labor market. Overall, train-

ing opportunities in relevant areas appear plentiful, but the quality of these opportunities has not been systematically assessed.

4.   While there is good coverage of high-demand fields in Qatar at the certificate/diploma level and undergraduate-degree levels, there are three notable gaps in the post-secondary offerings: limited opportunities for students who need remedial academic course work; limited choices in high-quality degrees in Qatar; and limited opportunities to study for a master's degree. These gaps differentially affect men and women, recent graduates and those who graduated some time ago, and highly able students.

CHAPTER SIX

Options for Providing New Educational Opportunities

In the last chapter, we identified three notable gaps in Qatar's available post-secondary educational opportunities that may require further investment, and we discussed the types of individuals who could benefit from the different types of expanded educational services. In this chapter, we first discuss our approach to arriving at the conceptual costs and benefits associated with each of the options for post-secondary investment. We then present the options for addressing the gaps and delineate the specific costs and benefits associated with each one. Our intent is to provide decisionmakers with guidance on how to prioritize possible investment in the three areas. Finally, we discuss the important need for coordination and long-term planning of investments in post-secondary education.

Conceptual Approach

Post-Secondary Investment Options

The options for investment for each post-secondary gap come primarily from areas of particular interest to Qatar's government. The SEC asked RAND to consider the following broad post-secondary investment options, which we have labeled SEC 1, 2, and 3 to establish a clear link to the specific investment options presented for each gap:

- SEC 1: Restructure programs at Qatar University.

- SEC 2: Recruit new foreign institutions to Qatar.
- SEC 3: Develop new government-sponsored post-secondary programs of less than four years.

These options focus on the provision of post-secondary programs in Qatar. The study abroad program and the scholarship system in Qatar, both of which are described in detail in Chapter Five, will continue to provide additional options for post-secondary education for qualifying students who are willing and able to go abroad.

Conceptual Costs and Benefits

To examine the conceptual costs of the various options, we adapted categories established in the literature on costs in education. As discussed in Cohn and Geske, 2004, the direct costs of education consist of costs paid by the school (e.g., for buildings, facilities, and faculty salaries) and costs incurred by students (e.g., for tuition, books and supplies, and transportation). In public universities, costs incurred by the school fall largely to the government; for private universities, students pay a greater share of the cost through tuition.

Conceptualizing costs is relatively straightforward because costs can be observed or measured fairly easily. For example, a post-secondary option that involves construction of a new building and facilities will be more expensive than an option that restructures degree programs without adding new infrastructure. Benefits of education, in contrast, are more difficult to conceptualize because they are to a certain extent subjective. What might be considered a benefit to one person, such as exposure to a new culture through study abroad, may not be considered a benefit to someone who values a more traditional education that reinforces the nation's cultural values.

Because of this subjectivity, the best way to learn about the value a society places on education is to ask individuals how they view educational benefits. To meet the requirements of this study, we relied on individuals' valuations of the benefits to both students and society of education in Qatar. This information came from the interviews with

Qatari employers and education leaders and the surveys we conducted during this study.[1]

Costs and Benefits of Post-Secondary Investment Options

This section presents investment options for each post-secondary education gap identified in Chapter Five, along with conceptual costs and benefits for each option. We focus on options that make sense for government policy rather than on every option that might be available to students.[2] Each discussion of the options, costs, and benefits associated with a post-secondary gap includes a summary table for ease of comparison across options.

Gap: Limited Opportunities for Remedial Course Work Prior to Admittance for University Study

Investment Option for This Gap

Establish a government-sponsored community college (SEC 3)

Benefits:

- *Remedial course work.* One of the missions of a community college is to provide the remedial course work necessary to prepare students to study for a four-year degree.
- *Open admission.* Government-sponsored community colleges are open to any secondary school graduate and therefore provide a "second chance" to prepare for university studies for students who

---

[1] The literature on the economics of education describes general benefits to an individual and society from education, such as lower crime rates and economic benefits from research (Schultz, 1963; Cohn and Geske, 2004). Many of these general benefits are not particularly relevant to Qatar, so we focused on the educational benefits specific to Qatar, as detailed in our interview and survey data.

[2] For example, a student might decide to hire a private tutor to better prepare for university admission or studies. This may be a useful choice for the individual, but it does not follow that government policy should support such an option.

struggled academically during secondary school and adults who have been out of secondary school for some time.

- *Flexible schedule.* Community colleges typically offer a flexible schedule of course offerings that allows individuals to take classes part-time while continuing to work or meet family responsibilities.
- *Credit transfer with Qatar University.* Course curricula at a government-sponsored community college and Qatar University can be coordinated so that students can transfer credits from the community college to Qatar University.
- *Broad mission.* Community colleges typically have a broader mission than a university does, and usually offer course work to improve general skills as well as academic skills. Therefore, even individuals not wishing to pursue a four-year degree could benefit from attending a community college.
- *Centralization of existing non-degree programs.* Current non-degree programs that support post-secondary education—typically remedial or preparatory programs such as the Qatar Foundation's Academic Bridge Program, Qatar University's Foundation Program, parts of Qatar University's Continuing Education Program, and the College of the North Atlantic's Access programs—could be centralized at a government-sponsored community college. Centralization would create administrative efficiencies by providing all college preparatory and remedial work at a single institution, and would allow the other post-secondary institutions to focus on their core missions. For example, Qatar University could focus solely on college-level training if the remedial work currently at the Foundation Program were shifted to a community college.

Costs:
- *Possible new infrastructure.* If no existing facilities and building were available, start-up infrastructure costs for a new building and facilities would have to be incurred.
- *Possible hiring of new faculty.* Some Qatar University faculty could teach at a community college, but it is likely that some new faculty would have to be hired.

- *Curriculum development.* New remedial-level curricula might have to be developed (or adapted from existing programs) to meet the needs of those not ready for university study.

Table 6.1 provides a summary of the benefits and costs associated with the option for remedial education.

The community college option holds promise for transforming post-secondary education in Qatar not only by meeting the need for college preparatory courses, but also by streamlining operations in current post-secondary institutions. These high-potential benefits may be costly, however. New buildings and facilities may need to be constructed to accommodate a community college, and new faculty may need to be hired.

While a new community college could fill a gap in Qatar's higher education system, it will not be a worthwhile investment if no one enrolls in it. Given the goals of Qatarization, many individuals could benefit from the kinds of education and training provided by a community college, but it is not possible to know whether the people it is intended to serve will actually enroll. It could, for example, be viewed as lacking prestige compared to Qatar University, making those it could benefit hesitant to enroll because there is a stigma attached to attending a community college. A full feasibility study is needed to determine the potential number of people who would attend a community college and the additional number of faculty that would be required.

Table 6.1
Summary of Benefits and Costs: Option for Remedial Education Prior to University Study

Option	Benefits	Costs
Community college	Remedial course work	Possible new infrastructure
	Open admission	Possible faculty hiring/training
	Flexible schedule	Curriculum development
	Credit transfer to Qatar University	
	Broad mission that meets needs of many	
	Centralized non-degree programs	

Part of the market segment that remedial education targets is adults, many of whom may have family and work obligations that make school costly. An important issue to consider is whether something can be done to ease the financial burden for adults who want to receive post-secondary education and training. One way to help alleviate the financial burden is to develop a financial aid program that is designed specifically to fund the post-secondary education and training of adults. This aid could take the form of scholarships for adults to attend post-secondary institutions, and vouchers that adults could use to gain training in high-demand areas (such as English and ICT; see Chapter Three for this subject). Recipients could use the funds for studies toward any type of academic degree, including studies at a community college (if one were to become available) and, perhaps, to pay for tutoring in preparation for college study. The vouchers could be used to receive training from a provider on an approved list, such as a list developed by the HEI. An attractive feature of a voucher program is that it allows individuals to pursue training wherever their needs are best met, including in the private sector.

Research on the feasibility of a financial aid program for adults is needed to assess whether there would be demand for such an option and, if there is, to work out the details of how it would work and how it would be coordinated with existing financial aid programs. As discussed in Chapter Five, the current aid programs target traditional, younger students.

Gap: Limited Four-Year Degree Choices for High-Achieving Students in Qatar Beyond Those Offered in Education City

Investment Options for This Gap

A. Recruit a top liberal arts college to Education City (SEC 2)

Benefits:
- *More high-quality degree choices locally.* Current Education City degrees are primarily in career-related fields (e.g., business, engineering, computer science). Establishing a top liberal arts college will provide more high-quality four-year degree options for

students, particularly women, who do not participate in study abroad.

- *General education service role.* A top liberal arts college could provide a service role in Education City by offering general education courses for the other Education City branch campuses that specialize in fields that are more career related. Each branch campus could then specialize in what it does best.
- *Enhanced regional prestige.* Establishing a top liberal arts college would make Education City more well rounded and may further enhance its regional prestige.
- *Improved English skills.* Offering more liberal arts courses in Education City would provide an experience very similar to studying abroad in the United Kingdom or United States and is likely to improve the English skills of students.
- *Improved preparation for graduate study.* Students who ultimately want to pursue graduate studies in the liberal arts will be able to receive strong preparation in Qatar before going abroad for graduate study.

Costs:
- *Start-up infrastructure.* A new branch campus in the liberal arts would likely require a new building and facilities.
- *Faculty and staff.* Faculty who agree to teach in the Education City branch campus would receive expatriate compensation packages, which include items such as salary bonuses, travel allowances, and housing allowances. Similar costs would apply for administrative staff.

B. Develop Qatar University Honors Program (SEC 1)

Benefits:
- *High-quality degrees in a traditional setting.* Some individuals and their families prefer a traditional, gender-segregated educational environment, which is not available in Education City. An honors program at Qatar University would provide a high-quality educational experience in a traditional setting. This is particularly important for high-achieving women who do not participate in study abroad.

- *Improved preparation for graduate study.* Students who go on to graduate studies will be better prepared to do so than current Qatar University graduates are.

Costs:

- *Curriculum development.* New honors courses would require that new curricula be developed, which could possibly include costs for hiring outside expertise.
- *Faculty professional development.* The faculty teaching in the honors program may need professional development, and external expertise may have to be hired to provide training.
- *Administration.* The new program will have administrative costs associated with hiring staff to support the faculty teaching in the program.

Table 6.2 summarizes the benefits and costs associated with the options for providing four-year degree choices.

Establishing a top liberal arts program in Education City has the potential to streamline the way in which post-secondary education is delivered in Education City. This option represents a major investment in infrastructure and faculty to provide the additional degrees and general education courses. The option of a Qatar University honors program would cater to the highest-achieving students at the Univer-

Table 6.2
Summary of Benefits and Costs: Four-Year Degree Choices for High-Achieving Students in Qatar

Option	Benefits	Costs
Top liberal arts college	More local high-quality degree choices	Start-up infrastructure
	General education service role	Expatriate faculty and staff
	Enhanced regional prestige	
	Improved English language skills	
	Improved preparation for graduate studies	
Qatar University honors program	High-quality degrees in traditional setting	Curriculum development
	Improved preparation for graduate studies	Faculty training
		Administrative

sity and represents considerably more modest costs than the option of establishing a new liberal arts institution. While the quality of a new campus of an established liberal arts college would, of course, be well known, the quality of a Qatar University honors program would be uncertain, at least in the short term, because the program would be a new enterprise. With time and sustained commitment from the Qatar University community, a good standing for the honors program may well be achievable.

Gap: Lack of Master's Degrees in Career-Related Fields in Qatar

Investment Options for This Gap

A. Expand offerings of current Education City campuses to include master's degrees in career-related fields. (Combines the program restructuring element of SEC 1 with the foreign institution element of SEC 2.)

Benefits:

- *High-quality graduate education in Qatar.* Students would receive an advanced education locally that is comparable to the education attained at top-tier universities abroad. This is particularly beneficial for students, typically women, who do not participate in study abroad.
- *Enhanced regional prestige.* Providing high-quality graduate education in Qatar would further establish Qatar as a regional leader in education.
- *Improved research capabilities.* Bringing top-tier graduate education to Qatar would increase the research done in country, which has the potential to benefit Qatar's industry and economy.
- *Improved English skills.* Students pursuing a graduate education in Qatar would improve their English language skills in a manner similar to that of top universities in the United Kingdom or United States.

Costs:

- *Some infrastructure.* Because the current Education City campuses have already built new buildings and facilities, no costs for these items need be incurred. However, some new facilities may be needed to support research.

- *Possible additional faculty.* More faculty may have to be brought in from the home campuses to support additional teaching and research and to mentor graduate students.
- *Some administration.* Additional support staff may have to be hired if current undergraduate support staff cannot take on the administration of the graduate programs.

B. Restructure Qatar University programs to begin offering more master's degrees in career-related fields (SEC 1)

Benefits:

- *Graduate education in a traditional setting.* Some individuals and their families prefer a traditional, gender-segregated education environment, which is not available at Education City. Graduate programs at Qatar University would provide a graduate-level educational experience in a traditional setting. This is particularly important for women who do not participate in study abroad.
- *Improved research capabilities.* Establishing graduate education at Qatar University would increase the country's research capacity, which has the potential to benefit Qatar's industry and economy.

Costs:

- *Some infrastructure.* Because Qatar University currently focuses on undergraduate education, some new facilities designed to support research may be needed if existing facilities can support only teaching.
- *Faculty professional development.* Because Qatar University faculty focus on teaching undergraduates, they may need professional development to enable them to teach and work with graduate students. There may also be a need to hire more faculty to support additional teaching and research, as well as to mentor graduate students. A short-term solution would be to hire visiting faculty on a temporary basis.
- *Some administration.* Additional support staff may have to be hired if current undergraduate support staff cannot take on the administration of the graduate programs.

A summary of the benefits and costs associated with offering master's degrees in career-related fields is provided in Table 6.3.

In contrast to the post-secondary investment options related to the previous two educational gaps, neither of these options requires major investment in entirely new infrastructure. Rather, both rely on expanding existing institutions to go beyond undergraduate education and provide master's degrees in career-related areas. The main difference between the two options is the quality of the master's programs provided. The master's programs at the Education City campuses are already well-established at U.S. campuses, and their high quality is virtually guaranteed. In contrast, the master's degree programs at Qatar University would be new and would take time to develop and become established. In addition, any plans for expanding Qatar University will need to be considered within the University's ongoing reform process. Currently, Qatar University's focus is on undergraduate education, with selected offerings at the master's level that reflect the University's current strengths and the nation's needs.

We do not recommend that a new foreign institution be recruited to Education City. Our inventory of post-secondary education and training offerings, discussed in Chapter Five, revealed that the current branch campuses in Education City provide exceptional opportunities for degrees in career-related fields that are in high demand in the labor market. Therefore, expansion of the existing programs to include master's degrees in career-related fields will fill this educational gap. We

Table 6.3
Summary of Benefits and Costs: Master's Degrees in Career-Related Fields

Option	Benefits	Costs
Master's degrees at current Education City campuses	High-quality graduate education in Qatar Enhanced regional prestige Improved research capabilities Enhanced English skills	Some infrastructure Possible additional faculty Some administrative
More master's degrees at Qatar University	Graduate education in traditional setting Improved research capabilities	Some infrastructure Faculty professional development Some administrative

also note that the study abroad program is still an option for students wanting to pursue graduate degrees, so the Qatar University graduate programs will be most relevant for those students who choose not to go abroad to study.

Coordination and Planning for Post-Secondary Education Investment

Along with the costs and benefits of the various post-secondary options, it is crucial to emphasize the necessity of developing an overarching, long-term plan for post-secondary investment. Any implementation of these options should be coordinated among the relevant institutions so that new investments mesh with the current post-secondary landscape. The options discussed in this chapter require coordination across multiple organizations, including the SEC, the Qatar Foundation, the HEI, and Qatar University. Our interviews with key employers and education stakeholders indicate that no such coordination mechanism currently exists.

Employer input may also be beneficial to the coordination and planning process in that it will aid in understanding potential labor market demand for new educational services. Moreover, labor market incentives and policies can affect educational choices. For instance, because men with a secondary education can find well-paying, secure jobs in the government (including in the police and military), they have few incentives to pursue post-secondary education. Labor market and employment policies may need to change if it is important that more men pursue post-secondary education in high-demand areas. In other words, providing more options may not, by itself, produce the desired results. As the Planning Council (2005) noted, Qatar currently lacks a labor market information system and the capacity for labor analysis or manpower planning.

Many of the options we have discussed for addressing post-secondary education gaps in Qatar are designed to fill the gaps on a large scale. However, it is worth mentioning that the results of a full feasibility study to assess the demand for these additional services may open the way for other options that are small scale and low cost. For example, if enrollment burgeons over time in high-demand fields, it may be more appropriate to increase class sizes, hire additional faculty, and/or add more sections of important courses than to establish a new institution. With careful planning and a full feasibility study, the scale on which to address the post-secondary gaps will become more evident.

CHAPTER SEVEN

Recommendations

Throughout this report, we have highlighted our key findings for each research question addressed by the study. In this chapter, we summarize our recommendations, including items for further consideration, based on those key findings.

Recommendation One

We recommend that the three gaps we identified in Qatar's current post-secondary education offerings be considered as areas for future investment, as follows:

- To address the gap resulting from the limited opportunities for remedial course work prior to admittance for university study, consider the option of establishing a government-sponsored community college. *Addressing this gap will benefit students not ready for college and adults.*
- To address the gap resulting from the limited number of four-year degree choices for high-achieving students in Qatar beyond the current Education City offerings, consider two options: (1) that of recruiting a top liberal arts college to Education City, and (2) that of developing a Qatar University honors program. *Addressing this gap will benefit high-achieving students.*
- To address the gap resulting from the lack of master's degrees offered in career-related fields in Qatar, consider two options: (1) that of expanding the offerings of current Education City cam-

puses to include master's degrees in career-related fields, and (2) that of restructuring Qatar University programs to begin offering more master's degrees in career-related fields. *Addressing this gap will benefit high-achieving students.*

Recommendation Two

We recommend that a financial aid program for adults be developed to help finance post-secondary education and training for adults.

Recommendation Three

Prioritization

We highly recommend that before any investments are made, Qatari policymakers prioritize the post-secondary gaps according to the value to be gained—by both the economy and the society—from addressing them. In doing so, policymakers should consider a number of issues, one of which is whether an investment addresses areas of national significance in furthering Qatar's economic and social goals. For example, providing high-quality graduate training will go a long way toward developing future leaders of the country, particularly women. The same reasoning applies to investing in new high-quality undergraduate programs. And community colleges may provide valuable training to many secondary school graduates not currently pursuing post-secondary education.

A second vital issue is the number and type of individuals that will benefit from the different investments. A community college could serve a wide segment of society, particularly those individuals who were not high-achieving students in secondary school. In contrast, investments in high-quality undergraduate education and graduate education will serve a relatively narrow segment of society—the most academically talented individuals. In a country such as Qatar, which has a small population, it is important to provide education and training opportunities to all types of individuals. However, which type of student takes priority at this time is a matter of strategic planning.

In prioritizing additional investment in local post-secondary education, it is important to consider the trade-off between students studying in Qatar versus studying abroad. Students can receive an education commensurate with their abilities through both of these forms of study, and each option has distinct advantages.

Feasibility Study

After determining the priorities for investing in post-secondary education areas, the next step is to conduct feasibility studies to determine with greater detail and specificity what is involved in investing in each area. Chapter Six discusses the conceptual benefits and costs associated with investment in the various options, but these are rather general, and a closer look at the detailed benefits and costs is needed. For example, if it is determined that more graduate education should be provided in Qatar, a feasibility study will help uncover exactly what would be involved in providing more graduate programs at Qatar University or what further investment would be required to enable Education City campuses to offer graduate degrees in Qatar.

The same issues are relevant to some extent for the other types of educational investments. Before investing in local graduate programs and additional high-quality undergraduate fields of study, the demand for such offerings among potential students needs to be determined. With respect to these two offerings, however, it needs to be noted that there are societal benefits associated with their provision, so the actual number who will take advantage of them may be somewhat less of a concern. For example, providing just a few Qataris with high-quality master's degrees will have the added advantage of preparing highly trained individuals who can take on the highest level of leadership in the country and who will serve as role models to young Qataris. Further, as discussed in Chapter Six, Qatar's regional prestige will be enhanced as other countries look to Qatar as the region's model for first-rate higher education. Having more graduate programs will also provide a more stimulating research environment in the country, which will benefit Qatar University and provide research and development for local industries. We make these points to illustrate that it is essential that the broader implications of the investments in post-secondary education be considered.

Conclusion

The development of Qatar's economy and society depends crucially on the education and training of its citizens. To develop a new generation of leaders who can continue to move Qatar forward in an increasingly global economy, Qatar must provide its young people with the best possible opportunities for post-secondary education and training. As this study has shown, in recent years, Qatar has invested heavily in post-secondary education—for example, in its establishment of both Education City, which provides top-tier education in selected fields in Qatar, and the HEI, which provides an opportunity for Qatari students to study at colleges and universities throughout the world. Qatar has been a regional leader in aggressively pursuing education reform at all levels, reforms that over time should contribute to building a more highly educated and thoroughly trained workforce and a more knowledgeable society.

This study has also shown that the post-secondary opportunities available in Qatar today are aligned with future employment demands, including employment outside the government sector. There are areas where Qatar's post-secondary education system can be developed further, however, and the study has detailed some specific ways in which Qatar's post-secondary education system can be strengthened through targeted educational investment.

Finally, this study has indicated that Qatari leadership must examine the investment options as part of the bigger picture. Although Qatar already provides many post-secondary education opportunities, enrollment rates for Qatari males remain low—partly because of the availability of secure, well-paying government jobs that do not require post-secondary qualifications. What this means is that the kinds of investment options discussed here may not, on their own, be able to change this pattern of post-secondary participation. Thus, any strategic planning with respect to post-secondary education must consider not only the educational landscape in Qatar, but also the labor and employment policies that may be working against the nation's educational goals. The leadership has supported a number of studies of the labor market (for example, an examination of ways to reduce the government sector) that may provide important information as strategic planning moves forward. Careful consideration of this study's recommendations, combined with broad strategic planning, should help in Qatar's development of the best educational opportunities for its future generations.

Study Approach and Methods

We relied on a number of different data sources in answering this study's research questions. We collected primary data through three methods: a set of formal and informal interviews with employers in the broader public and private sectors, telephone interviews with a sample of Qataris who had left secondary school in 1998, and surveys filled out by a sample of secondary school seniors who were at least 18 years of age. We also carried out an inventory of post-secondary education institutions and training establishments. Secondary data sources included census and labor market data reported by the Planning Council, additional interview data from prior and concurrent RAND studies, and data provided by the HEI. This appendix discusses our data collection procedures and analyses for these different data sources.

Employer Interviews

Employers

We sought to gather views from a range of employers, to include the public and private sectors and roughly in proportion to the distribution of Qatari employees over these sectors. As only 2 percent of Qataris are employed in the private sector (Planning Council, 2005), most of the formal interviews were carried out in organizations belonging to the broader government sector.

It is useful to understand the differences in the types of organizations that make up Qatar's public sector, in which most Qataris are employed. There are four types of governmental entities:

1. *Ministries:* Purely governmental agencies that follow the employment regulations of the Ministry of Civil Service Affairs and Housing (MoCSAH).
2. *Authorities:* Service-focused, non-profit entities funded by the government (e.g., Civil Aviation authority).
3. *Councils or supreme councils:* Publicly funded entities that reflect the government's current area of policy focus. They are usually headed up by one of the nation's leaders and enjoy independent status as to setting salaries and budgets.
4. *Public corporations:* For-profit entities that are assigned an initial budget, which is treated as starting capital, by the government. Some provide public services for which they charge but are not set up as commercial profit centers. Although they have the potential to turn a profit, none do (e.g., Hamad Medical Corporation, Q-Post, Kahramaa). Others are set up as commercial profit-making entities for the government, are self-managed, and, if successful, can offer shares to the public (e.g., Qatar Petroleum, Aspire, Qatar Airways).

As discussed in Chapter Two, labor market analyses distinguish between corporations fully and partly owned by the state, referring to those partly owned as constituting the "mixed" sector. In addition, the private sector includes establishments that are fully privately owned or are at least 51 percent Qatari-owned in some industries.

Sample Selection and Procedures

We first developed a list of candidate organizations in the public and private sectors. We approached each organization to set up interviews with an executive, sometimes the human resources manager, and in some cases a supervisor of frontline employees. Typically, interviews were conducted by at least two members of the research team, one conducting the interview while the other took notes. In a few cases, the executive invited the human resources manager or a staff person involved in training. Interviews varied from about an hour to a half-day presentation and question-and-answer period that included six staff holding different roles (e.g., executives, supervisors, trainers). Formal interview notes were entered into ATLAS.ti, a text management program, and coded by interview question.

The interview guidelines for the executive protocol were designed to gather information related to the main study questions and to cover a variety of topics, including: types of knowledge, skills, and attitudes needed in high-demand occupations; whether applicants have necessary skills; hiring and advancement of female employees; types of jobs open to secondary school and post-secondary graduates; workforce characteristics (gender, nationality); skill differences between Qatari and non-Qatari employees; training and other strategies for acquiring skills; extent to which strategies are successful; and connections to education (e.g., knowledge about current education reforms, activities with schools). Supervisors were asked similar types of questions, with more emphasis on the specific job skills needed and less emphasis on organizational strategy.

Respondents participated under conditions of confidentiality and are therefore not named or directly quoted in this report. Table A.1 shows the organizations interviewed and the number of respondents.

Survey of 1998 Secondary School Graduates

In March 2006, trained researchers conducted the survey of 1998 secondary school graduates by telephone. We chose the 1998 cohort because these individuals, in 2006, would have had eight years of experience since graduating from secondary school. This time frame allowed us to examine transitions from secondary school and from post-secondary education or training into the labor market.

Survey Design
The survey gathered background information (e.g., gender, marital status) and included questions about employment and educational

Table A.1
Formal Interviews Conducted

Organization	Type of Organization	Respondent (No.)
Ministry of Interior	Ministry	Executive (1)
Qatar Armed Forces	Ministry	Executive (1)
SEC Evaluation and Education Institutes	Council	Executive (2)
Supreme Council for Information Technology	Council	Executive (1)
MoCSAH	Ministry	Executive (1)
Hamad Medical Corporation	Public corporation	Executive (2); supervisor (1)
Qatar Petroleum	Public corporation	Executive (1); supervisor (4)
Qatar Airways	Public corporation	Executive (1)
Qatar National Bank	Public corporation	Executive (1); supervisor (1)
Sheraton Hotel Doha	Private company	Executive (1)

background and current status. In addition, a supplemental form was developed that targeted currently unemployed people to take a deeper look at the reasons behind their unemployment, their needs, and the obstacles they faced.

The main questionnaire first asked for demographic information, including marital status and number of children, and then asked about labor market histories, including the respondent's current employment status and number of jobs held since graduating from secondary school. We then asked respondents who had ever held a job a series of questions pertaining to their first and their most recent jobs, including: type of employer (e.g., government ministry, government enterprise), job title, and job duration. For the most recent job, we also collected information on how the respondent found out about the job, minimum level of education required, specific skills required by the job, and extent and type of training respondent received to learn these skills.

The next part of the main questionnaire asked about attitudes toward work and schooling. One battery of questions was on the importance of particular job characteristics in determining choice of career. The second set of questions asked whether the respondent agreed with a series of statements about school and work.

The final portion of the main questionnaire was on education. We collected information on current level of schooling and school enrollment, as well as on plans for pursuing additional education. For individuals who only completed secondary school, we asked about their reasons for not pursuing additional schooling. For respondents who did go on to post-secondary school, we asked for the type of school (e.g., vocational or four-year), major field of study, and whether a degree was received.[1]

The supplement for those not employed was designed to collect information on the experiences of individuals who chose not to work or who were unable to find a job they thought suitable. It asked whether the respondent was looking for work and, if so, what barriers they were facing in looking for a job. For respondents not looking for work, we asked about their reasons for choosing not to be in the labor force.

The survey was developed in English, pilot-tested by each interviewer, revised by the team, translated into Arabic, and then (for analysis purposes) back-translated into English.

Sample Selection and Procedures

The population from which we drew our sample comprised students who had graduated from secondary school in 1998. To identify these individuals, we used data from the Ministry of Education that contained a record for each individual who registered for the 1998 Secondary School Exit Exam (those who register are primarily from government schools, but students at the Religious Institute, the Industrial Institute, and private Arabic schools also register). Students who failed the 1998 exit exam did not graduate in 1998, so we only sampled from the set of students whose exit exam records indicated they had successfully passed (some students who failed may have passed and graduated at some later date; they would not have been included). Out of 2,620 students who took the exit exam in 1998, 1,881 passed. Of these, 676 were male (36 percent) and 1,205 were female (64 percent).

---

[1] We collected this information for the first and the most recent post-secondary school the respondent had attended.

Our goal was to administer the survey to 50 men and 50 women from this population. We used a strategy of random sampling with replacement, which ensured that each individual had an equal probability of being selected. We first drew an initial sample of 450, which was reduced to 399 after deleting duplicate names. Of these, 146 were males and 253 were females. Each name was given an identification number and randomly assigned to an interviewer on the research team of the same gender. Each interviewer had a target number of interviews to complete based on his or her time availability during the data collection period. Each went down his or her list until the target number of interviews had been completed.

Interviewers made a maximum of three attempts to reach any one person on their list using the phone number provided by the Ministry of Education as a starting point. The attempts took place over different times of the day and over at least two different days. The timing of the calls took into consideration local working hours, local weekends, and other social factors. If after three attempts the interviewer had failed to reach the person, or to conduct an interview, he or she documented the facts and moved on to the next name on the list. Ultimately, we were able to complete 99 anonymous interviews, 50 with males and 49 with females. All interviews were conducted in Arabic.

Representativeness of Sample

The exit exam database includes information on the student's secondary school field of study. We can assess the representativeness of the interviewed sample by comparing the distribution of field of study in the population to that observed in our sample. The results, shown in Table A.2, suggest that the sampled individuals are reasonably typical of the overall population, at least in terms of secondary school field of study. Females who studied science or literature, math, and science are slightly under-represented, and females who studied French literature are over-represented. For males, the proportions of students specializing in a particular field are very similar in both the sample and the overall population.

Table A.3 compares the sample's percentage of individuals having more than a secondary degree with that in the 2004 census. To approx-

Table A.2
Field of Study, 1998 Survey Respondents and All 1998 Secondary School
Graduates, by Gender

	Percent Women		Percent Men	
	Population	Sample	Population	Sample
Science	30	24	38	40
Literature, math, and science	52	47	52	50
French literature	18	29	2	0
Industrial	0	0	5	8
Commercial	0	0	2	2
Religious studies	0	0	0	0

SOURCE: Authors' calculations based on Ministry of Education exit exam database and survey responses of 1998 cohort.

imate the population from which we drew the sample, we restricted our attention to individuals in the census who were age 25 to 29 and had at least a secondary degree. Note that even with this restriction, the census and survey sample are not completely comparable, since not all individuals in the 1998 cohort were age 25 to 29 at the time of the 2004 census. However, this is the closest comparison that can be made. The results suggest that the women in the sample may be somewhat better educated than women in the overall population, with 79 percent of women in the sample having more than a secondary degree compared to 61 percent in the census. In contrast, the rate of postsecondary schooling for men is nearly identical in the sample and census (51 percent in the sample and 46 percent in the census).

Table A.3
Those with More Than a Secondary Degree, 1998 Survey
Respondents and 2004 Census Figures, by Gender

	Percent with More Than a Secondary Degree	
	Sample	2004 Census
Males	51	46
Females	79	61

SOURCE: Authors' calculations based on 1998 cohort survey responses and published tabulations from 2004 census (Planning Council, 2004). Census figures refer to Qataris age 25–29 with at least a secondary degree.

Analysis Approach

To analyze these data, we made comparisons of sample means and pro-portions across different groups identified in the data. For instance, we made extensive comparisons of the responses of males versus females and, because they were particularly relevant to policymakers, the responses of individuals who had pursued post-secondary schooling and those who had not. Where appropriate, we used standard statisti-cal tests (e.g., t-test, chi-square test) to see if differences across groups were statistically significant. A significance level of 5 percent was used throughout.

As noted previously, we sampled an equal number of males and females even though there are more females than males in the sampling universe.[2] For analysis purposes, the survey responses are weighted to adjust for the proportion of males and females in the population. Specifically, the sample weight for female respondents is equal to the ratio of the share of females in the population to the share of females in the sample: $(1205/1881)/(49/99) = 1.29$. The weight for males is $(676/1881)/(50/99) = 0.71$.

Survey of 2006 Secondary School Seniors

Survey Design

The student survey was designed to gather information about second-ary school students' educational and career aspirations, and about the factors that may affect those aspirations. The survey began with back-ground questions, including date of birth, gender, nationality (Qatari or non-Qatari), course of study, current grade, year in current grade (first time or repeating), and father's and mother's level of education.

The second part of the survey asked students about their plans for the future, such as what they planned to do directly after graduat-ing from secondary school, and what factors affected those plans (e.g., parental advice, religious beliefs, societal expectations).

---

[2]   Note that the population in this case refers to all individuals in the Ministry of Education database who were seniors in 1998 and passed the exit exam.

Students were also asked several questions about work and careers, including what type of job they would like to have, the preparation they would need to reach their career goal, and the type of organization in which they would like to work (e.g., government, government enterprise).

Students were also asked about the importance of different job characteristics to their choice of job, such as salary, work environment, benefits, and about the factors that might help or prevent them from achieving their career goals. Finally, we asked students for their opinion on a number of statements about school and work. These items were partly designed to gather some empirical data that could support or refute opinions of employers and others about what motivates young Qataris. For example, prior RAND studies identified a prevailing view that Qataris, especially men, were mostly motivated by salaries and prestige and preferred jobs with shorter working hours (Brewer et al., 2007). These items also tapped attitudes about women and work, an important policy issue in Qatar as the government seeks to increase women's workforce participation.

The draft survey was written in English, translated into Arabic, and then back-translated into English. A member of the research team pilot-tested the survey. The Arabic version of the survey was administered in all schools.

Sampling Strategy

We employed a random sampling strategy, stratified by school gender and school type, to select 11 secondary schools that represent the diversity of schools in Qatar. The sample included four Ministry of Education schools, two generation I Independent schools, three generation II Independent schools, and two private schools. Definitions of these different types of schools are as follows:

- Ministry of Education schools operate under the direct supervision of Qatar's Ministry of Education.
- Independent schools are publicly funded and operate under contract to the SEC's Education Institute. Part of a recent K–12 education reform, the generation I Independent schools opened

in September 2004, and the generation II Independent schools opened in September 2005.

- Private schools are fee-charging education organizations licensed by the Ministry of Education but otherwise not subject to direct oversight.

After the list of schools was generated, we used a database containing names of students in their third year of secondary schooling in each Ministry of Education, Independent, and private Arabic school to identify those students in each school who would be 18 years of age or above at the time the survey was to be administered. A list of student names for each school was generated and sent to the school's principal, who set aside a classroom in which to administer the survey. A member of the study team administered the survey to all eligible students who were in attendance on the day of the survey administration. Participation was voluntary and anonymous. Virtually every student agreed to participate. Due to scheduling conflicts, one of the private schools did not participate. In all, 260 students—106 males and 154 females—completed the survey.

The first item of the survey asked for date of birth, which allowed us to double check that all participants were at least 18 years old. By surveying only students age 18 and older, we avoided the process of obtaining parental permission. Given the short time span and other demands of the larger study, we were concerned that the parental-permission process could cause delays in data collection. It also seemed unlikely that by singling out 18-year-olds, rather than surveying seniors of all ages, we would bias the results in any meaningful way. As it turned out, most principals informed the selected students' parents about the survey, and no objections were raised.

The survey was closed-ended except that students were asked to write in the kind of job they would most like to have. These written responses were translated into English, and completed surveys were sent to RAND's Survey Research Group for data entry.

Sample Weighting

Survey responses were weighted to reflect the distribution of 18-year-olds across the different types of schools in Qatar. We used data from the Ministry of Education to determine the number of 18-year-olds during the period of the survey administration across all school types in Qatar. We constructed weights using the following formula:

$$ w_S = \frac{1}{N} \frac{a_S^{POP}}{a_S^{SAMP}} \,. $$

Each student observation is weighted by w_S, with s representing the school that the student is enrolled in. N is the sample size, a_S^{POP} is the share of students enrolled in school s to the total population of students (who were 18 and above during survey administration), and a_S^{SAMP} is the share of students in school s to the total sample of students. A student from a school that was over-sampled relative to the population was weighted down because that student represented a larger share of the sample, and vice versa for students who were under-sampled. These weights were used in calculating descriptive statistics for the survey responses where appropriate.

Table A.4 shows the population characteristics of the school types and the calculated weights.

Table A.4
Population Characteristics of School Types and Calculated Weights

Type of School	Total Number of Qataris Meeting Criteria		Number in Sample		Calculated Sample Weight	
	Males	Females	Males	Females	Males	Females
Private Arabic	21	122	6	NA	0.005072464	NA
Ministry of Education	580	674	73	111	0.011514791	0.008250098
Independent, generation I	5	10	4	7	0.001811594	0.001940994
Independent, generation II	84	52	23	36	0.005293006	0.00196256
Total	690	858	106	154		

Coding of Job Titles Written in by Survey Respondents

Both surveys asked respondents to write in a job title.[3] We classified these jobs into 11 categories using the scheme laid out in ISCO-88. Most occupations were combined according to ISCO-88's "major groups," or the "one digit level."[4] In some cases, however, a relatively large number of job titles fell into a common occupation grouping below the "major group" level. Our results therefore separately identify these finer groupings: associate professional, engineer, military/ police, and teacher. Table A.5 shows the 11 categories we used and gives two illustrative examples of unedited job titles that we put in each category.

Table A.5
Occupation Categories and Examples of Unedited Written-In Job Titles

Occupation Category	Unedited Job Title
Associate professional	Legal research, assistant librarian
Clerk	Administration (assistant), business permit inspector
Elementary	Security supervisor, security man
Engineer	Engineer, chemical engineer
Legislator/senior officer/ manager	Management or business, management
Military/police	Police officer, Emiri guard
Operator	Operator, senior operator
Professional	Accountant, lawyer in military affairs
Service worker	Store keeper, makeup artist
Teacher	Teacher, art teacher
Technician	Technician I, manual technician

---

[3]   The survey of the 1998 secondary school graduates asked respondents to write in the title of their first and their most recent jobs. The survey of the 2006 secondary school seniors asked respondents to write in the job they would most like to have.

[4]   The International Labour Organization's ISCO-88 classification system is at http:// www.ilo.org/public/english/bureau/stat/isco/isco88/index.htm (as of May 23, 2007). Elias and Burche (1994) provide additional information and definitions of the terms used in the occupational groupings.

Inventory of Post-Secondary Institutions

Data on institutions that grant post-secondary degrees were gathered in April through June 2006. We contacted the deans from Virginia Commonwealth University, Texas A&M University, Weill Cornell Medical College, Carnegie Mellon University, Georgetown University, College of the North Atlantic, and CHN University Netherlands, and the Office of Institutional Research and Planning at the University of Qatar, and all agreed to participate by completing a short open-ended survey that asked for various pieces of institutional information. The information we requested included number of enrolled students for each year the institution had been in operation and number of graduates (where applicable) by nationality and gender, as well as freshman year retention rates and time to degree (where applicable). Information about courses and degrees offered was also requested, as was information about the institutions' formal and informal relationships with employers and any career services offered to students. Most institutions submitted the requested data within two weeks; two required follow-up via phone calls.

Data on training providers were gathered in May through June 2006. From a sample of training providers recommended by the employers interviewed for this study, we selected five to interview by phone. They were asked for basic institutional information, such as year established, number of students served per year, number and qualifications of instructors, relationships with employers, and course offerings and certification programs. Obtaining data from training providers proved to be difficult over the telephone, since some organizations were reticent to provide such information without first verifying the source of the request. In response to training providers' requests, we arranged in-person interviews with three of them. A member of the study team conducted these interviews with the directors of the institutions or their designated representatives.

The inventory data provided the input for answering the third study question, as discussed in Chapter Five.

Secondary Data Sources

The main secondary data sources consulted for this study were the 2004 census and two labor force studies sponsored by the Planning Council (2002, 2005). These provided broad information on characteristics of the labor market, such as distribution of the workforce by gender, nationality (Qatari, non-Qatari), industry, occupation, and educational credentials. These data shed light on who was working in occupations considered vital to Qatar's economy and society both now and in the future.

To supplement the surveys and interviews conducted as part of this study, we also reviewed information about education, employment, training and skill needs gathered in numerous prior and ongoing RAND studies. The electronic note files from these studies were systematically reviewed and summarized by key topics. By drawing on these interview data we reduced the burden on institutions and individuals who had been previously visited.

The HEI provided a third source of secondary data. We asked the HEI to provide information about its scholarship programs, including the number of students enrolled in each of the scholarship programs and associated costs.

Post-Secondary Degrees Offered in Qatar

Institution and Date Established	Degrees Offered

Virginia Commonwealth University–Qatar, 1998	Bachelor of Fine Arts in:
	    Graphic design
	    Interior design
	    Fashion design

Weill Cornell Medical College–Qatar, 2002	Doctor of Medicine (program includes mandatory 2-year non-degree-granting pre-med program)

Texas A&M–Qatar, 2003	Bachelor of Science in:
	    Electrical engineering
	    Mechanical engineering
	    Chemical engineering
	    Petroleum engineering
	(Master's degrees in engineering and science are to be offered starting in 2007)

Carnegie Mellon University–Qatar, 2004	Bachelor of Science in:
	    Business administration
	    Computer science

Georgetown University–Qatar, 2005	Bachelor of Science in foreign service

CHN University Netherlands–Qatar, 2000	Bachelor of Arts in:
	    Hospitality management
	    Tourism management

College of the North Atlantic–Qatar, 2002	Diploma and certificate programs in:
	    Engineering
	        Chemical laboratory technician
	        Electronics eng. tech., communications
	        Electronics eng. tech., power and control
	        Industrial instrumentation technician
	        Mechanical engineering technology
	        Mechanical technician
	        Telecommunications eng. tech.

Institution and Date Established	Degrees Offered
	Business
	Office administration certificate
	Office administration, executive
	Office administration, records and info. mgmt.
	Banking and finance
	Business administration, financial accounting
	Business administration, human resource mgmt.
	Business administration, marketing
	Business management, financial accounting
	Business management, human resource mgmt.
	Business management, marketing
	Health Sciences
	Environmental health
	Medical radiography
	Pre-nursing
	Primary care paramedicine
	Respiratory therapy
	General
	Information Technology
	Computer support specialist
	Internet application developer
	Programmer analyst
	Information technology
	Trades
	Security preparatory training
	Technician training program
University of Qatar, 1973	***College of Education***
	Bachelor of Arts in:
	Fine arts education
	Physical education
	Post-graduate diplomas in:
	General education
	Special education
	College of Arts and Sciences
	Bachelor of Arts in:
	Arabic language and literature
	History
	Geography and urban planning (double major, males only)
	Social work
	Sociology
	Information and library science
	Mass communication

Institution and Date Established	Degrees Offered
	Bachelor of Science in:
	Mathematics
	Biological sciences
	Physics
	Computer science
	Chemistry
	Statistics
	Geology (males only)
	Agricultural science (males only)
	Biomedical science (females only)
	Food science and nutrition (females only)
	College of Sharia and Islamic Studies
	Bachelor of Arts in Sharia and Islamic studies
	College of Engineering
	Bachelor of Science in:
	Chemical engineering
	Civil engineering
	Electrical engineering
	Mechanical engineering
	Computer engineering
	Computer science
	Industrial and systems engineering
	College of Business Administration
	Bachelor of Arts in:
	Accounting
	Economics
	Business administration
	Public administration (military program)
	Master's in business administration
	College of Law
	Bachelor of Arts in:
	Law
	Law and Sharia

Training Providers in Qatar

Provider	Year Est. and Type	Average Number of Students per Year	Type of Students	Relationship with Employers[a]			Examples of Employers	No. of Full-/Part-Time Instructors and Degs. Held	Offerings for Adults	Certifications and Diplomas
				FA	TT	OT				
New Horizons	1999, for-profit	1,000	Individual residents	x	x	x	Qatar Foundation, Qatar Petroleum, Dolphin, municipalities	25/5, B.A.'s	Certification prep. classes (3 mos., 2–4 hrs/day) for International Computer Driving License (ICDL), Microsoft Certified Systems Engineer, Microsoft Office Specialist, CISCO, Oracle, At, 3-D Max, Autocad, MS Project	*New Horizons diploma in Administration:* 1-yr full-time program (2–4 hrs/day, 5 days/wk) that includes courses in time mgmt., office mgmt., filing, workplace behavior, basic economics and statistics, etc. *Other diplomas:* Public Relations and Marketing, Office Mgmt., Basic Computer Maint. and Troubleshooting
ELS	1997, for-profit	4,800	Individual residents, corp. and govt. employees	x	x		Qatar Petroleum, Qatar Fertilizer, Qatar Steel Co., Qatar Telecom. Co., Planning Council, Independent schools, govt. agencies	2/51, B.A.'s	Intensive English (3 hrs/day, 4 days/wk, 4 wks); Business English (1.5 hrs/day, 3 days/wk, 4 wks); Financial English; English for Executives; Test of English as a Foreign Language prep. (3 hrs/day, 4 days/wk, 4 wks)	*British Council certificates in English Proficiency*

Provider	Year Est. and Type	Average Number of Students per Year	Type of Students	Relationship with Employers[a]			Examples of Employers	No. of Full-/Part-Time Instructors and Degs. Held	Offerings for Adults	Certifications and Diplomas
				FA	TT	OT				
Expert	2005, for-profit	30–35	Govt. employees	x	x	x	Various govt. agencies	NA/NA, B.A.'s (from various local univs. in Cairo)	Courses in accounting, admin., mgmt., safety, law (typically 1 wk long, offered in Egypt 2 times/yr)	None
British Council (Teaching Centre)	1972 (in Qatar), not-for-profit	5,000–6,000 part-time	Individual residents, corp. and govt. employees	x	x	x	Govt. orgs., private-sector orgs., Independent schools	NA	General English; Business English; International English Language Testing System prep. courses; Cambridge First Certificate in English prep. courses (typically 2 hrs/day, 2 days/wk, 8 wks [regular term] and 1.5 hrs/day, 5 days/wk, 4 wks [summer])	*British Council–level certificates* (Univ. of Cambridge Local Exam Syndicate suite of English as a Foreign Language exams available as supplement)

Provider	Year Est. and Type	Average Number of Students per Year	Type of Students	Relationship with Employers[a]			Examples of Employers	No. of Full-/Part-Time Instructors and Degs. Held	Offerings for Adults	Certifications and Diplomas
				FA	TT	OT				
Hi Tech	1994, for-profit	1,000	Individual residents, corp. and govt. employees	x	x		Kahramaa, Carrefour, Qatar Gas, hotels, Al Jazeera, Independent schools	9/2, B.A.'s	English Language, 6 levels (48 hrs each; typically 2 hrs, 3 times/wk); prep. courses for ICDL, proficiency in various computer programs (12–48 hrs, typically 3 times/wk for 2 hrs)	*Hi-Tech international diploma:* a 6-mo program for women that covers basic English language skills, comm. skills, general office and financial mgmt.

[a] FA = formal agreement, TT = training tailored for employer, and OT = on-site training offered.

References

Bailey, Thomas R., Katherine L. Hughes, and David Thornton Moore, *Working Knowledge: Work-Based Learning and Education Reform*, New York and London: RoutledgeFalmer, 2004.

Brewer, Dominic J., Catherine H. Augustine, Gail L. Zellman, Gery Ryan, Charles A. Goldman, Cathleen Stasz, and Louay Constant, *Education for a New Era: Design and Implementation of K–12 Education Reform in Qatar*, Santa Monica, Calif.: RAND Corporation, 2007. As of April 30, 2007:
http://www.rand.org/pubs/monographs/MG548/

Central Intelligence Agency, *World Factbook*, Washington, D.C.: U.S. Government Printing Office, 2007. As of May 10, 2007:
https://www.cia.gov/library/publications/the-world-factbook/print/qa.html

Cohn, E., and T. Geske, *The Economics of Education*, 3rd edition, Mason, Ohio: Thomsen South-Western, 2004.

Economist Intelligence Unit, "Country Profile 2004, Qatar," London, 2004.

Elias, Peter, and Margaret Birch, *Establishment of Community-Wide Occupational Statistics: ISCO 88 (COM), A Guide for Users*, University of Warwick Institute for Employment Research, February 1994. As of May 23, 2007:
http://www2.warwick.ac.uk/fac/soc/ier/research/isco88/englishisco.doc

Foreign Information Agency, State of Qatar, "Higher Education and Health: Higher Education," undated. As of May 1, 2007:
http://english.qatarinfo.net/topics/index.asp?cu_no=1&operation_type=6&item_no=487&version=1&template_id=305&parent_id=303

Gause, F. Gregory, *Oil Monarchies: Domestic and Security Challenges in the Arab Gulf*, Washington, D.C.: Council on Foreign Relations Press, 1994.

Higher Education Institute, Scholarship Guide 2006–2007, June 12, 2006. As of April 30, 2007:
http://www.english.education.gov.qa/content/announcements/detail/3585

Institute of International Finance, Inc. (IIF), *Summary Appraisal, Gulf Cooperation Council Countries*, August 15, 2006.

Nafi, Z. A., *Economic and Social Development in Qatar*, London and Dover, New Hampshire: Francis Pinter, 1983.

Organisation for Economic Co-operation and Development, *From Initial Education to Working Life: Making Transitions Work*, Paris: OECD, 2000.

Planning Council, State of Qatar, *Sample Labour Force Survey, April 2001*, Doha: Planning Council, State of Qatar, 2002.

——————, *2004 Census*, Doha: Planning Council, State of Qatar, 2004. As of May 23, 2007:
http://www.planning.gov.qa/Census_2004/population/index_e.htm

——————, *A Labour Market Strategy for the State of Qatar: Main Report*, Vol. 1, December 2005.

Qatar Foundation, "Education City Qatar: The Future," Web page, updated January 23, 2007a. As of April 30, 2007:
http://www.qf.edu.qa/output/page304.asp

——————, "Vision and Mission: History," Web page, updated January 25, 2007b. As of April 30, 2007:
http://www.qf.edu.qa/output/page294.asp

——————, "Student Services: Financial Aid," Web page, updated February 22, 2007c. As of April 30, 2007:
http://www.qf.edu.qa/output/page383.asp

——————, "Student Services: Student Employment Program," Web page, updated February 22, 2007d. As of April 30, 2007:
http://www.qf.edu.qa/output/page378.asp

Qatar Ministry of Foreign Affairs, "Oil and Gas," Web page, undated. As of May 24, 2007: http://english.mofa.gov.qa/newmofasite/details.cfm?id=15

Qatar University, "The Reform Project," 2006. As of June 20, 2007:
http://www.qu.edu.qa/html/reformproject.html

Schultz, T., *The Economic Value of Education*. New York: Columbia University Press, 1963.

Secretary's Commission on Achieving Necessary Skills, *What Work Requires of Schools*, Washington, D.C.: U.S. Department of Labor, 1991.

Stasz, Cathleen, "Assessing Skills for Work: Two Perspectives," *Oxford Economic Papers,* Vol. 3, 2001, pp. 385–405.

Stasz, Cathleen, Kimberly Ramsey, Rick Eden, Hilary Farris, Julie DaVanzo, and Matthew W. Lewis, *Classrooms at Work: Teaching Generic Skills in Academic and Vocational Settings*, Santa Monica, Calif.: RAND Corporation, 1993. As of April 30, 2007:
http://www.rand.org/pubs/monograph_reports/MR169/

Stasz, Cathleen, Kimberly Ramsey, Rick Eden, Elan Melamid, and Tessa Kaganoff, *Workplace Skills in Practice: Case Studies of Technical Work*, Santa Monica, Calif.: RAND Corporation, 1996. As of April 30, 2007:
http://www.rand.org/pubs/monograph_reports/MR722/

Supreme Education Council, "Fact Sheet on Higher Education Institute," press kit, March 16, 2005. As of May 1, 2007:
http://www.english.education.gov.qa/content/resources/detail/1543

U.S. Census Bureau, "IDB Summary Demographic Data for Qatar." As of May 23, 2007:
http://www.census.gov/cgi-bin/ipc/idbsum.pl?cty=QA

U.S. Library of Congress, "A Country Study: Qatar," in Helen Chapin Metz (ed.), *Persian Gulf States: Country Studies*, Federal Research Division, Library of Congress, 1994. As of May 24, 2007:
http://lcweb2.loc.gov/frd/cs/qatoc.html

Winckler, Onn, *Population Growth, Migration and Socio-Demographic Policies in Qatar,* Israel: Moshe Dayan Center for Middle Eastern and African Studies, Tel Aviv University, 2000.